THE INSPIRED POET

Writing Exercises To Spark New Work

SUSAN LANDGRAF

Two Sylvias Press

Copyright © 2019 Susan Landgraf

All rights reserved. No part of this book may be reproduced in any form without the written permission of the publisher, except for brief quotations embodied in critical articles and reviews.

Two Sylvias Press
PO Box 1524
Kingston, WA 98346
twosylviaspress@gmail.com

Cover Artist: Denise A. Schroeder, *Three Abstract Whales*
Cover Design: Kelli Russell Agodon
Book Design: Annette Spaulding-Convy
Author Photo: Lisa Nichols

Created with the belief that great writing is good for the world, Two Sylvias Press mixes modern technology, classic style, and literary intellect with an eco-friendly heart. We draw our inspiration from the poetic literary talent of Sylvia Plath and the editorial business sense of Sylvia Beach. We are an independent press dedicated to publishing the exceptional voices of writers.

For more information about Two Sylvias Press please visit: www.twosylviaspress.com

First Edition. Created in the United States of America.

ISBN: 978-1-948767-07-1

Two Sylvias Press
www.twosylviaspress.com

Praise For *The Inspired Poet*

An engaging and generous personal writing guide, sure to inform and inspire.

— Kim Addonizio, author of *Ordinary Genius: A Guide for the Poet Within*

※

One of the most difficult aspects of the writing life is simply getting started: quieting our internal critic long enough to create a first draft. With this diverse series of craft-focused, creative-writing exercises, Susan Landgraf offers the keys to unlock the writing inside us—and the fuel to inspire the writing that sustains us.

— Jordan Hartt, author of *Leap* and *Drifting*

※

Susan Landgraf is indeed paying attention, and with this collection of playful, engaged, provocative exercises, she makes us pay attention as well—to cages and bodies and blankness and song, to cream of wheat, letters to our feet, and apple slices under a virgin's arms, and mostly to the poems waiting to be born inside, outside, and all around us.

— Sam Ligon, author of *Among the Dead and Dreaming*, *Safe in Heaven Dead*, *Wonderland*, and *Drift and Swerve*

※

Writers, your subconscious installs writer's block into your wetware to rescue your work from a wrong turn. Your personal "keep writing" tricks can't crack it. Remember when writing was more fun than frustration? Try other writers' tricks to break your block and to bring fun back to your writing. Susan Landgraf's *The Inspired Poet* offers breakthrough tools from, and for, writers of all genres. Writing is serious business, but never forget: Fun is good! Use it!

— Bill Ransom, author of *The Woman and the War Baby* and *Jaguar*

INTRODUCTION

The Inspired Poet, which comes out of years of teaching and leading workshops, offers writing exercises, prompts, poems, and facts for poets, teachers, workshop leaders, and prose writers. They are meant to be invites for the Muses to come visit.

Even if you're not a poet and don't like to write, these invites might entice you to see yourself and the world in a new light. This book may give an insight into grief or a respite from grieving for something or someone lost—or for celebrating something found.

The exercises in *The Inspired Poet* can be used for your personal writing practice, for writing groups, leading poetry workshops, and in the classroom. Both novice writers and established writers can find inspiration in the 37 chapters of this book, each of which offers unique exercises on such topics as structure, pop culture, revision, mythology, grief, relationships, nature, symbolism/imagery, women's voices, psychology/sociology, and personal reflections on creativity/inspiration.

The chapters in *The Inspired Poet* can be completed in any order—move from the first chapter to the last in succession or jump around, depending on your creative whim. These chapters vary in length and number of exercises, so you can pick chapters accordingly—in-depth, detailed exercises for an all-day workshop, or if you are time-crunched, chapters that can be completed more quickly.

As with all writing exercises and prompts, it's important for you to *feel inspired*, so please adapt these exercises so that your creativity is sparked with ideas for new poems. Also note that there is no wrong way to respond to an exercise—the chapter on childhood memories may lead to a poem about an event last week that has nothing to do with your childhood, and that's absolutely fine. The goal of *The Inspired Poet* is for you to create new poems for chapbooks and manuscripts or for your own satisfaction from bringing your ideas and feelings onto the page.

I craved light growing up in a basement in Ohio with an unpredictable and violent birth father. I listened to *The Lone Ranger* on the radio and wished he would come save my mother, two sisters, and me. That didn't happen. Books saved me then – and my mother's parents.

Later, love and friends and poetry saved me.

In David Wojahn's essay "Can Poetry Save Your Life?" published in *Blackbird*, he states at the beginning that "sad to say, no," poetry can't save lives. (He does add that it might have saved "Ben Jonson, the great Elizabethan poet and playwright.") Wojahn concludes by saying that he endorses what John Berger, who wrote *Ways of Seeing*, says about poetry.

Berger wrote that poems "bring a kind of peace. Not by anesthesia or easy reassurance, but by recognition and the promise that what has been experienced cannot disappear as if it had never been… The promise is that language has acknowledged, has given shelter, to the experience."

Wojahn writes that "that promise" didn't save him but that it sustains him and gives him comfort.

Is that not, in a mad, mad world, a gift?

Gregory Orr, on the other hand, believes poetry can save us. Poetry saved him. After accidentally killing his younger brother, Orr wrote in *this i believe* that out of that horror–"grief, terror, shame and despair… I found something to set against my growing sense of isolation and numbness: the making of poems." In his piece for NPR, "The Making of Poems," Orr said it is both the act of being "the maker of poems" and of being the reader of others' poems: "The gift of their poem enters deeply into me and helps me live and believe in living."

I hope you, too, will be the maker of poems and the reader of other's poems.

Susan Landgraf, 2019

TABLE OF CONTENTS

Chapter 1: Childhood Inspiration—Yer A Wizard, Harry / 1

Chapter 2: Proverbs, Idioms, And Clichés—Oh My! / 6

Chapter 3: Acrostics / 10

Chapter 4: With A Little Help From The Stars / 14

Chapter 5: Structure—Shaping A House To Hold The Poem / 18

Chapter 6: Ads Everywhere / 22

Chapter 7: Blank Spaces And Quiet / 26

Chapter 8: Color Outside The Lines / 32

Chapter 9: My Body, My Poem / 36

Chapter 10: Connotations / 41

Chapter 11: The Trickster Coyote / 47

Chapter 12: Writing Into Our Fears / 53

Chapter 13: Write Your Townscape / 58

Chapter 14: Po-Jack 101 / 63

Chapter 15: It's A Piece Of Cake / 68

Chapter 16: You Can Quote Me / 75

Chapter 17: When Grief Inspires / 81

Chapter 18: Invent-A-Word / 86

Chapter 19: Fact Or Fiction? / 92

Chapter 20: You Can't Write About Love / 96

Chapter 21: Leaping Poetry / 99

Chapter 22: Outside And Inside Out / 104

Chapter 23: In Praise Of Everything / 108

Chapter 24: Questions Without Answers / 111

Chapter 25: The Shapes In Our Poems / 116

Chapter 26: Seedlings And Starts / 119

Chapter 27: Thinking In Similes / 124

Chapter 28: Looking At All Sides / 128

Chapter 29: Follow Your Nose / 132

Chapter 30: Leave No Stone Unturned / 136

Chapter 31: Who Or What Is Your Muse? / 139

Chapter 32: The Poet And The Sea / 144

Chapter 33: Sounding Life Into Your Poems / 149

Chapter 34: Women's Voices In The World / 155

Chapter 35: Connect The Dots / 164

Chapter 36: Revisioning / 169

Chapter 37: Concluding Thoughts—Why Poetry? / 177

Contributor Bios / Poem Permissions / 183

About The Author / 191

This book is dedicated to:

Lonny Kaneko, Carl Sandburg and all my teachers.

all of my writing family, some of whose poems are included in *The Inspired Poet*.

my family—Brett Landgraf, Ted Landgraf, Jennifer Landgraf and Lisa Nichols, their significant others—Donna Landgraf, Dion Maxwell, and Dennis Nichols—and my grandchildren and great grandchildren. The count is 48 at this time; I'm grateful for them all.

and all those I love—you know who you are.

Chapter 1: Childhood Inspiration—
Yer A Wizard, Harry

As adults we are profoundly influenced by our childhood experiences, and these, in turn, influence who we are and how we respond to the world. Do we ever truly leave our childhoods behind? The truth is: the child we were is always in us, whether we see her or pay attention to him or not.

How do we let that child speak?

Heather Sellers, author of *The Practice of Creative Writers*, states: "Children and artists, it's often said, are more alike than different." If you let that child out, you might find, as Sellers says, that "Art, like children, asks questions." And you may see that sense of curiosity and wonder coming out on the page.

Exercise 1: List Poem

Make a list of how you saw the world as a child. Maybe clouds looked like giraffes and elephants or you thought the stars were little lights hung in the sky. Maybe you were inspired by the books that you read and imagined yourself to be certain characters. Some of these memories might be surreal and may not make logical sense—your pets talked to you or you thought your uncle was really a pirate. Try to list at least seven ways that you saw the world; use specific details.

Use your list to write a "list poem" of how you saw the world as a child. A list poem is exactly as the title implies—a poem that is a list of things. Sometimes list poems use repetition, especially at the beginning of each line: "because" or "I am" or "tomorrow." Christopher Smart was an 18th century poet who wrote a list poem titled "Jubilato Agno" about his cat. Here are a few sample lines from his lengthy poem to give you an idea of how a list poem works:

For I will consider my Cat Jeoffry.
For if he meets another cat he will kiss her in kindness.
For when he takes his prey he plays with it to give it a chance.
For one mouse in seven escapes by his dallying.
For he is of the tribe of Tiger...

Exercise 2: Real And Imagined Facts

List five questions you had as a child and then write a poem that answers one of your questions. For example, you might have wondered: Do leaves want to be the first one to fall from the tree or do they want to be the last to fall?

Use some facts in your poem to answer your question. To answer the question about autumn leaves, you might use one or more of the following scientific facts:

> Leaves are green because of chlorophyll.
> When leaves change color they produce a fractal-like pattern.
> Water and carbon dioxide create simple sugars.
> When temperatures cool, cork cells form at the base of each leaf.

You can also include some of your own imaginative theories about a leaf's desire to fall:

> If you're first to fall, the ground is harder.
> If you're last to fall, you're likely to be lonely.
> How long you stay on the branch depends on the wind and how thick your skin is.
> The longer you stay attached to the branch, the fewer birds there are to sing to you in the morning.

Interweave in your poem both the scientific facts and your own imaginative theories to answer your childhood question.

Exercise 3: Places I Remember

Write a poem about a place you remember as a child—a place you loved or a place you hated. Give details about who was there with you, what the place smelled like, whether it was sunny or raining, etc. Observe the place and you in it, and describe what you were doing, what you were feeling. Try to avoid using abstract terms like "I was scared" and instead, show your reader what exactly, in detail, caused you to be frightened ("the door to the attic would creak and pop loudly when it was windy outside..."). Consider writing your poem as a prose poem, not worrying about line breaks. Your finished poem will have the shape of a small paragraph. Also, try to write your poem without a lot of internal editing—allowing images and memories to rise spontaneously from your subconscious.

Poems To Inspire Your Work:

AMERICAN LAKE

Always in my hand
when I was a kid,
fireworks in a brown bag:
Black Cats, Ground Bloom
Flowers, Black Snakes.
I wore maryjanes
and an organza dress,
pink with teeny flowers.
Everyone was in the house,
eating potato salad
and Aunt June's jelled surprise.

I lit a firecracker,
dropped it into an empty
glass pop bottle–
a muffled explosion
and shards blowing
outward, but each,
missing me,
slivered the air.

I stayed outside, quiet,
holding my fireworks.

by Ann Spiers

୮ଚ

UMBILICAL
for my mother

Not flesh but string, the line which bound your foot
To mine, hobbling me so you could nap
And not worry I would wander loose
Those summer afternoons. But who could sleep

In such light? No boy of eight. I'd wait
Until your breath grew even. Holding mine,
I'd sit up slowly, carefully work the knot—
A ball of snake coils small but intricate
As trip-wires. One day I slipped the noose,
eased off the creaking bed. I felt my face
Tighten around the eyes. Afraid you'd call
Me back, I tiptoed toward the doorway: no sign
I'd wakened you. I listened, then took a step
Through—and saw the darkness of the long hall.

by Michael Spence

ဢ

MALIBU BEACH
   —for my brother Joey

What if there were no light, he wondered. Just sound & scent owning the night,
    without the invasive

Surf Shop green neon, or PCH streetlamps glowering at everyone.
Their glint was wrong, false, while the waves sounded
like aloe on a burn, a quick fix.
Some blue & some red lights also flooded the water—flashed

onto a surfer. *Someone's riding the barrel! Ricky? Anton? Robbie?* he couldn't tell—
they were all blond or blondish, lean. Kids.
If he were out there & they were
bent over this squad car, arms pinned back, cuffs cold & final,

those dudes could name him—stupid dark, stupid stocky, stupid
curls intense against his skull.
If he were out there, he'd Hit-the-Lip & hang a Soul-Arch,
a quick fix.

The water, when it was clean, could fix anything.
If he were out there he wouldn't be 18 with his face away from the seaweed
    breeze, with his face
shoved into a back seat.
His sister's voice floated up from the water, "Wherever you go

there you are." *Well, I'm not
going to jail,* he thought as he was driven from the pilfered Surf Shop,
    the Pacific. *I'm going to
ride a killer pipeline in Oahu.* He was sure he'd get to
the past present future

torrent of the pacific in every direction.

by Jennifer Jean

Chapter 2: Proverbs, Idioms, And Clichés—Oh My!

Before humans could read or write, they passed knowledge by word of mouth. Many times these sayings have been recited to us by parents or grandparents, or perhaps, we've said them ourselves. Benjamin Franklin published *Poor Richard's Almanack* from 1732 to 1758 to share his knowledge. Here are a few sayings from Franklin's many "truths":

> A penny saved is a penny earned.
> An ounce of prevention is worth a pound of cure.
> Fish and visitors stink after three days.
> Little strokes fell great oaks.
> To err is human, to repent divine; to persist devilish.
> Well done is better than well said.

Here is a short list of a few of proverbs and idioms that have been passed down one way or another:

> A stitch in time saves nine.
> A bird in the hand is worth more than two in the bush.
> A sound mind lives in a sound body.
> All work and no play makes Jack a dull boy.
> Don't judge a book by its cover.
> Don't judge a man until you walk a mile in his shoes.
> If it ain't broke, don't fix it.

The following quotes come from *Aesop's Fables*, a collection of fables written by Aesop, a slave who lived in Ancient Greece during the 5th century BCE. There are more than a hundred fables credited to Aesop.

> Things are not always what they seem.
> Familiarity breeds contempt.
> One person's meat is another's poison.
> Slow and steady wins the race.

Many times clichés offer some well-believed truths and advice:

> All that glitters isn't gold.
> And they all lived happily ever after.
> Read between the lines.
> Only time will tell.
> A diamond in the rough.

Every cloud has a silver lining.
Don't cry over spilled milk.
It's the calm before the storm.
Laughter is the best medicine.
She's head over heels in love.

Exercises 1: Time Flies, but Sometimes It Walks

Choose a saying from any of the lists above, and write a poem where, in your opening line, you offer an exception, such as "A penny saved is a penny earned, / except when it's dropped in the gutter…" or "Things are not always what they seem, /except when they are exactly what they seem…" Your poem can then move into any topic, but feel free to return and reuse your original line in different variations at any time in the poem.

Exercise 2: Grandma Always Said…

Think about the first time you heard one of the adages above (or choose one of your own). Try to remember who said it and under what circumstances. For example, I remember my grandmother, after she heard a church member criticizing another church member, say, "People who live in glass houses should not throw stones." She often said, "It's more blessed to give than to receive." (Acts 20:35)

Write a poem where you return to that experience. Make sure to focus on the details and use specific images to show the era in which it took place (for example, black and white TVs bring us back to the 50s and 60s while permed hair bring us into the 70s and 80s, etc.) Also, you may consider writing the poem in the voice of the person who said it as a commentary about life.

Exercise 3: Argue With A Saying

Choose a saying and write a poem as an argument against the nugget of truth you've chosen. For example, instead of "You can't judge a book by its cover," start with "You *can* judge a book by its cover;" or, if you choose "Slow and steady wins the race," write a poem that begins with "Fast and chaotic wins the race."

As you write, allow humor and wit to enter the poem. Get into an argument with the saying you choose or suggest new and better interpretations. For example, not only does fast and chaotic win the race, but sometimes drunk and lazy or lost and kooky wins. These poem responses to well-known sayings offer many opportunities to add a bit of play into your work.

Poems to Inspire Your Work:

JUDGE A BOOK BY ITS COVER

If you can't judge a book by its cover,
then every cover should be generic white
with black lettering titled *Poetry Book:
Metaphors and Rhymes Included.*

The word *judge* has such a bad rap:
rhymes with budge and grudge. We're stuck
in sludge with Mudge the begrudging pudge

who won't nudge. *Judge* doesn't eat sweet fudge.
She's blind and tasteless, balances
truth like a bored waitress carrying crepes.

The letters in *judge* need to stretch out
on a yoga mat, raise themselves into downward
facing dog, arch their backs to breathe in
the world though its senses.

by John Davis

☙

IN HAWAII, WE DO THIS

No one wanted to
hold my hand at Brighton Elementary
when the wart appeared at the base
of my ring finger. It was lumpy with ridges
like the barnacles speckling
ocean stones. I wore bow-tied dresses

with pockets, keeping my fist closed.
And under pressure, in the damp heat
of my fingers, the wart dug in and grew.

The doctor's glowing punk
couldn't burn hot or deep enough. Maybe Dad
saw that I believed more in frog spit
and the harsh words of my friends.
In Hawaii, my father said, *we do this*
and his knife split the eggplant. Two tear shapes
fell to the sides. Dad rubbed the juice
into my hand. Then I followed him
to the far corner of our backyard
where the day seemed dim. No one
would believe me, I thought, as we buried
the eggplant. I smelled the earth
as Dad's shovel tamped it down. He nodded
with the rhythm of his words: *When this rots,
your wart will die and fall off.* All the way
back in to dinner, he held my sticky hand.

by Sharon Hashimoto

Chapter 3: Acrostics

We look at our world in increments to help us make sense of everything around us: seconds, weeks, months, etc. We make lists, create timelines, write outlines. We have routines and rituals to give ourselves a map, some insight and order.

An acrostic is a poem, or other form of writing in an alphabetic script, in which the first letter, syllable or word of each line, paragraph or other recurring feature in the text spells out another message. For our purposes, an acrostic is a poem in which the first or last letter of each line spell out a word, phrase, or name. The word "acrostic" comes to the English language via the Latin derivation of the Greek words "akron" (end) and "stikhos" (line of verse).

Acrostics are both poems and puzzles. Some people love putting puzzles together—finding the little tabs, corners, or a line that connects with others to finally create a full image. Others like crossword puzzles or Sudoku. Some say reading maps is like interpreting a puzzle. And others of us puzzle our way into a line or image or poem for our brainwork of the day.

Acrostics have been written in many languages: Greeks of the Alexandrine period, Latin playwrights, and medieval monks and poets. Edgar Allan Poe wrote "An Acrostic" that used the name Elizabeth. Lewis Carroll in *Through the Looking-Glass* included an acrostic called "A Boat, Beneath A Sunny Sky" that spelled out Alice's full name: Alice Pleasance Liddell (the inspiration for *Alice's Adventures in Wonderland*).

Exercise 1: Acrostic Name

Write an acrostic name poem by choosing the name of a person you admire (fictional, famous, a friend, or a relative) and write his/her name (first and/or last) vertically down the left side of your page.

For example, if you choose Eleanor Roosevelt as your person you would arrange the letters in the following format:

E
L
E
A

N
O
R
R
O
O
S
E
V
E
L
T

Your poem might begin with something like this:

Every child in the 1930s looked up to you
Learning by your example of treating
Each person you encountered with dignity...

This acrostic poem can be about anything, but think about including hints or images that represent the person you have chosen. Your poem can also directly honor or praise your subject. You do not have to capitalize each letter at the beginning of the line—the choice is yours.

Exercise 2: Acrostic Phrase

For this acrostic poem, think about a short phrase that states how you are feeling at this moment or some truth that you try to live your life by. For example "I am nervous," "Life is fantastic," "Love to all around me," "Do no harm," etc.

Write the first letter of each word at the beginning of each of your lines:

D
O
N
O
H
A
R
M

Now, create a poem that either directly or subtly addresses the phrase you have chosen. For instance if you use the phrase "I am nervous" maybe write about that upcoming root canal that has you dreading the appointment. Also feel free to break your phrase into couplets or triplets or other stanzas.

Poems To Inspire Your Work:

VOICE OVER

Create
Understanding,
Luscious
Thunderstorms
Invigorating
Vigor
And whatever else we can
Take from the knowledge of those
Incandescent clouds that hob
Nob with whatever gods (no
Gender ascribed, please) will have us.

Voice is something to use
Over and over
In remarkable volumes,
Creating chords from
Empathy.

by Sandra Yannone

∞

PURSUITS
Nothing makes a man so adventurous...
  – Victor Hugo

Entropy in the garden, but eggplants
make efforts to stand tall amidst weeds.
Perfection's a myth we lean toward to
tantalize ourselves – carrots beyond reach.
Yesterday I found myself letting a deadline slide
past like a wedding cake yacht; on deck, smart
occupants tipped chins toward sunbeams, sipped
champagne from flutes, and nibbled canapés.
Knots in laces force me to slow my pace, to
exercise patience. Deer wait, peaking from shadows
to let sugars rise in all my green, aspiring sprouts

by Katrina Roberts

&

AN ACROSTIC

Elizabeth it is in vain you say
"Love not" — thou sayest it in so sweet a way:
In vain those words from thee or L.E.L.
Zantippe's talents had enforced so well:
Ah! if that language from thy heart arise,
Breath it less gently forth — and veil thine eyes.
Endymion, recollect, when Luna tried
To cure his love — was cured of all beside —
His follie — pride — and passion — for he died.

by Edgar Allan Poe

Chapter 4: With A Little Help From The Stars

Some people wake up every day and read their horoscopes while other people don't put too much belief in their astrological sign at all. Below is some general information about horoscopes to get you started

The horoscope dates vary a bit, depending on the source, but these dates are common:

>Aries 3/21 - 4/19
>Taurus 4/20 - 5/20
>Gemini 5/21 - 6/21
>Cancer 6/22 - 7/22
>Leo 7/23 - 8/22
>Virgo 8/23 - 9/22
>Libra 9/23 - 10/22
>Scorpio 10/23 - 11/21
>Sagittarius 11/22 - 12/21
>Capricorn 12/22 - 1/19
>Aquarius 1/20 - 2/18
>Pisces 2/19 - 3/20

Here are a few words associated with each sign:

>Aries—initiating, daring, energetic, reckless, impatient, headstrong
>Taurus—earthy, practical, patient, possessive, stubborn, lazy
>Gemini—intelligent, sociable, inventive, shallow, inconsistent, nosy
>Cancer—emotional, sensitive, domestic, insecure, overprotective
>Leo—self-confident, radiant, creative, prideful, egocentric, vain
>Virgo—organized, economical, meticulous, picky, judgmental, petty
>Libra—cooperative, balanced, harmonious, indecisive, dependent
>Scorpio—imaginative, idealistic, visionary, chaotic, delusional, mean
>Sagittarius—wise, visionary, adventure, zealous, dogmatic, scattered
>Capricorn—cautious, responsible, hardworking, stubborn, brooding
>Aquarius—unconventional, innovative, independent, erratic, odd
>Pisces—compassionate, imaginative, sacrificing, impractical, chaotic

This was a daily overview (Scorpio) from Yahoo Celebrity's site: "You reach a significant fork in the road today, yet your current map isn't clear about where either path leads. Unfortunately, your decision-making process is a lot more complicated now because of this ambiguity. Nevertheless, the Moon's shift into your sign later in the day triggers your final answer, emboldening you to paint your future...and you can't go wrong."

Find today's horoscope online or in your local paper and read the different horoscopes to inspire the exercises below.

Exercise 1: Her Leo Courage and Aries Temper

Write a poem about a relationship using words from one or several of the signs. Integrate them in this poem as you search for insight or understanding about your situation. Choose a form for your poem that mirrors the relationship—for example, if you are writing about a spouse or lover, write in couplets; if you are writing about you and your parents, write in 3-line stanzas.

Exercise 2: It's Your Lucky Day

Write a poem where you take your horoscope advice for the day and respond to it. You might try a bit of sarcasm, irony, humor, or wit. Feel free to allow the poem to move into surrealism or magical realism to add even more surprise. Maybe your horoscope suggests that travel is in your near future, so your poem takes the reader into a fantasy land, or perhaps space travel to a planet is involved. For extra credit, use the name of an astrological sign in your title or last line.

Exercise 3: Should a Goat Marry a Fish?

Write a poem where two people with different signs interact with each other. Consider having their astrological signs be an important part of the poem—maybe have them look/act like their astrological sign. For example, maybe a Pisces swims up to a Capricorn standing on a rock. Another idea is to think about the sign of a person you are in a relationship with (partner, child, friend, coworker, etc.), and write about how your personalities either complement each other or cause chaos.

Exercise 4: The Astrologer Is In

Pretend you are an astrologist giving advice to someone who has come to you with a question or a specific fear. Maybe they are afraid that the world has become dangerous or maybe they need help with their marriage. Write a poem that incorporates several descriptive words from each sign or is written as a positive horoscope for the person who is asking the question. Give them the advice they need. A title idea may be the name of the sign and what question they are trying to solve, for example, "Advice to the Gemini Looking for Love."

Poems To Inspire Your Work:

DEAR HOROSCOPE WRITER

First, what does significant mean? A fork,
you say: I've often been at forks where
of course I was conflicted. Of course the decision-making
process is complicated. It's this not knowing. And
though the Moon's shift should trigger my answer,
I ask you: In this part of the country this time
of the year with rain, rain, and more rain, with leaves
flying in every direction, you really think I'm going
to see the moon, much less be emboldened to make
a decision. What do you mean I can't go wrong?
Being out in the wind and rain at this fork, all I want is
my bed, and lemon and honey with my whiskey.

by Susan Landgraf

☜

HOROSCOPE

Chinese Horoscope: Born 1973, the Year of the Ox –
Sincere, persevering, stubborn, intelligent.
Born in April under Taurus, the Bull,
headstrong, material, another working stiff.

But how can a horoscope say anything about you?
laughing, he asks me, *Can everyone born
in the same week, in the same year have similar traits?
Ridiculous*, he shrugs, *even to suggest it.*

But here I am, weighted down by my intractable
horns, pushing you out of your shell,
little Crab, little Cancer...
as we build a nest from earth and water.

by Jeannine Hall Gailey

Chapter 5: Structure—Shaping A House To Hold The Poem

If you build a house, the house rests on its foundation (unless you didn't measure and didn't know what you were doing, which means the house may fall down). And, of course, you don't want to build your house on sand.

If you paint on a canvas, the size of the canvas influences what you paint. The neck of a bottle determines what you put in it. A wooden box can't hold fire for long.

Here are some general guidelines on poetic structure:

> Stanzas shift the poem just as paragraphs do in a story—the more you have, the more "characters" or moves you have in the poem.
>
> A block of text gives a view that holds together, like a window that shows everything in one pane of glass.
>
> Lines that span most of the page tend to offer a "story" approach.
>
> Short lines tend to be brisk or more didactic.
>
> Punctuation and line breaks make a difference not only in rhythm but in how we approach the poem. Caesuras (a break in a verse where one phrase ends and the following phrase begins) make us slow down or look more closely.

Exercise 1: Structure 8 Ways

Write a poem on any topic using one (or more) of the following suggestions as a way to structure your work:

> —an "ed" or "de" or "st" or "ts" or "er" at the end of each line of your poem
> —a long line or short line format
> —use questions only, no direct statements
> —write with no punctuation and/or just one long sentence
> —each line enjambed (break the line at place where there is no punctuation)
> —each line end-stopped (each line ends with a period)

—use repetition: choose a word or phrase to use at least three times
　　　that changes meaning or shifts the poem in some way
　　　—use numbers, statistics, or measurements throughout your poem

This exercise can be one or several exercises. You can use each of these examples as one way to structure your poem or you can combine them.

Exercise 2: Couplets, Tercets, and Quatrains

Write a poem about a relationship using only couplets or tercets or quatrains.

Couplets have two lines per stanza. Couplets imply pairing, but you also could use juxtaposition: one line about light, the other about dark.

Tercets are three-line stanzas. Sometimes poets choose this form to write about topics that come in threes. Tercets essentially have three legs to stand on, sometimes three different directions, but all tied together–a beginning, a middle, and end.

Quatrains were, at one time, the most popular stanza form along with couplets. Many narrative poems were written in this form. Quatrains use four-line stanzas and tend to offer a larger canvas and a sense of fullness.

Choose the stanza structure that works the best for your topic. You can also write the same poem in different stanza structures to see how it changes.

Poems To Inspire Your Work:

DIFFERENT PLACES TO PRAY

Everywhere, everywhere she wrote; something is falling–
a ring of keys slips out of her pocket into the ravine below;

nickels and dimes and to do lists; duck feathers from a gold pillow.
Everywhere someone is losing a favorite sock or a clock stops

circling the day; everywhere she goes she follows the ghost
of her heart; jettisons everything but the shepherd moon.

This is the way a life unfolds: decoding messages from profiteroles,
the weight of mature plums in late autumn. She'd prefer a compass

rose, a star chart, text support messages delivered from the net,
even the local pet shop–as long as some god rolls away the gloss

and grime of our gutted days, our global positioning crimes.
Tell me, where do you go to pray–a river valley, a pastry tray?

by Susan Rich

☙

THIS MORNING
Light takes the Tree; but who can tell us how? – Theodore Roethke

It's time. It's almost too late.
Did you see the magnolia light its pink fires?
You could be your own, unknown self.
No one is keeping it from you.

The magnolia lights its pink fires
daffodils shed papery sheaths.
No one is keeping you from it—
your church of window, pen and morning.

Daffodils undress, shed papery sheaths—
gestures invisible to the eye.
In the church of window, pen and morning
what unfolds at frequencies we can't see?

Gestures invisible to naked eye
the garden opens, an untranslatable book
written at a frequency we can't see.
Not a psalm, exactly, but a segue.

The garden opens, an untranslatable book.
You can be your own unknown self—
not a psalm, but a segue.
It's time.

by Elizabeth Austen

WHEN I CONSIDER EVERYTHING THAT GROWS
After William Shakespeare's Sonnet #15

To gaze upon nature in her bounty
Her beauty transient as a falling star.
All the world is nothing but illusion,
A conjuring slight like lantern magic.
Seeing how the human race thrives
Even as it swells and so must shrivel
Prideful in their prime, but waning too soon.
Splendid, their ephemeral plumage,
The very thought gives pause.
You bloom before my eyes,
Though I know we too must wither
Just as primrose petals fold at dusk;
Forever shall I keep you nigh
Even as our eyes grow dull, my words your lifeblood.

by Beverly Osband

Chapter 6: Ads Everywhere

The average American sees 5,000 or more commercial impressions in a day. All of these commercials are intent on impressing and on selling. They rely on sex, fear, and death in one way or another. They stimulate their audience by attracting attention—for instance electronic media often uses violence and special effects. I taught media classes for twenty-seven years, and in the last dozen or so years, one of my assignments required students to keep track of their media consumption for a full week—everything they watched or listened to or any actions they performed, from surfing on the internet to playing video or computer games; from texting to emailing to working on a word document. This also included any movies or shows that they watched as well as any music they listened to. Students were shocked at the percentage of each day they spent on or with media and how much of what they consumed came through advertising.

There are two tactics. *Hard-sell* is time-dependent: Buy this car or SUV or truck now while you can get a rebate. Shop this week because bananas are on sale. *Soft-sell* is based on desire and want. You would be so much happier if you had _____ (fill in the blank).

Most Americans spend an average of 58 hours a week using media (radio, television, internet, game console, phone, tablet, Pandora, Netflix, etc.). Mass media now gives the average American small bites. When TV was live, some companies, such as Texaco, bought thirty-minute or sixty-minute blocks of time for their advertising. By the 1990s, ads were down to fifteen seconds each, and the ads were targeted to a particular audience—different ads in the morning, for instance, compared to ads shown in the evening. Today, ads on YouTube are sometimes only five seconds long.

Exercise 1: Is Love An Iced Mocha Or A Prius?

Look carefully at five advertisements (internet, magazine, newspaper, etc.) and make a quick list of words that describe each ad. Choose five words from each of your five descriptions, and use these words in a poem about an abstract concept, such as love, hate, sadness, joy, freedom, or loss.

Here is an example poem that I composed:

Freedom

To buy silk, effervescence
and wrinkle-free everything. Angora's good, a cherry-red
Jaguar with the top down
under a diamond-studded sky.
A king out of the movie-reel jungle
who'll arch his eyebrow, who'll know, of course,
the ropes. I'll feel silky
under his touch when he carries me
to Paris, marking the days until the Tiffany-style,
golden and unbelievably beautiful wedding.

Exercise 2: Taste The Rainbow

Choose one of the ads that you studied for Exercise 1 or choose a new ad, and write a poem about what the ad evokes within you—what you see and feel when looking at it. Does a Trojan condom ad bring up a certain sexual experience? Does a Honda ad remind you of the thrill you felt driving the first time by yourself? Does the Advil ad give you a sense of hope or relief? Does the MacBook Air ad make you feel like your computer is slow and out of date? Let your chosen ad speak to you; dig into memories, beliefs, and wants. Limit your poem to fifteen lines.

Exercise 3: Zero-Down And Bold

Prompted by six to ten of the following words that were chosen from random contemporary ads, write a poem choosing one of the following prompts:

   —Try to sell something in your poem.
   —Revisit a childhood memory, such as a wagon, your favorite book, a
      telescope, a game, a glow-in-the-dark ring, etc.
   —Describe something about the natural world.
   —Paint an image of how you see our current society.

Here is your list of words from various advertisements:

quick, zero-waste, delivered, latest styles, upgrade, savings, live-streaming, discover, proven, sexy, unique, opportunity, zero-down, bold, promise, smartest, lite, selective, dedicated, balance, focus, future, unlimited, fast, hybrid, roar, reimagined, reinvented, boundless, highly-anticipated, solutions, exclusive, magic, authentic, elegant, uninterrupted, on-demand, indulgence, engineered, perfection, thrive, power, organic, answer, next generation, secure, rugged, all-new, explore, tasty, convenient, smooth, energy, no-carb

Poems To Inspire Your Work:

RE-BRANDING

First—   the tramp stamp
(a Ulysses butterfly with broken wings
she will later extend to cover the entirety of her back).
Her forearm next—
                    a lily pad.
                    A knife
covers a name she regrets
on her right breast.
Her shoulder blade—
a Chinese symbol
for penitence.
            A Nigerian proverb
for, worry not
about tomorrow,
snakes up her thigh
            and under
her skirt.
No other language
has roughed her up
to let her know who's boss
the way English has,
            the way English lied
with a straight face, told her
if you learn me, I'll protect you.
She feels pretty now
and safe
scarred in symbols
that haven't failed
her yet.

by Jamaica Baldwin

IN THE SELF-HELP AISLE

she had *Mixed Feelings*, but she knew *What You Feel You Can Heal*,
so she decided it was time to *Find a Husband at 35*. He was sitting

in Nature & Outdoors, an excellent specimen. *Sex, Money, and Power*,
she thought, but first she needed to thumb through *Exhibitionism*.

for the Shy, get past her *Shining Affliction*, consider *Men, Women,
and Relationships*. This could take awhile, but if she focused on

The Art of Thinking, this *Sleepwalker Wakening* might not have to
Migrate to Solitude to win her affections. Then she spied it –

the telltale wedding band. So that's why he paid no mind!
He must know *The Secrets of a Very Good Marriage*,

Finding the Love, but then again any second he could reach
above her, loosen *The Good Divorce* from between the clutches

of *Emotional Unavailability* and *The Transformative Power
of Crisis*. But no, he seemed happy enough with his nose inside

The Voyage of the Beagle, which gave her the chance to settle into *Joy
in the Everyday, Making Peace with Yourself, Composting a Life*.

by Martha Silano

Chapter 7: Blank Spaces and Quiet

What is a blank space, or as some writers and designers call it, *white space?*

W. S. Merwin in his poem "To the Blank Spaces" wrote *white lakes on the maps,* while Linda Pastan in "Consider the Space Between Stars" wrote about blank space as *the space between thoughts.*

In poetry more white (or blank) spaces help us navigate the poem rather than slogging through it. Gary Lehmann, who teaches writing and poetry at the Rochester Institute of Technology, claims that most pages of poetry consist of 1% print and 99% white space. He adds, *White space should be a vital part of every poet's vocabulary.*

Sometimes in modern art, you can have a twelve-foot canvas with a small dot in the lower right corner and a green dot in the upper left corner. Think about the paper or word document as a canvas, and consider the many ways you can format you poem on the page to explore the idea of "white space."

Do you always put one space between stanzas? What if you put four spaces between? Do all your lines look alike. What   if you spread   your line across the page   with spaces   like this? You have many ways to play with space in your poems.

And as you continue to read poems, watch for the various ways poets use space in their work.

Exercise 1: Make It Concrete

Write a poem about a cloud (or something else in nature) or an urban environment that can exist on its own visually. Consider ways to use the white space of your paper or document to feature the image you are writing about. If you write about clouds, can you format the poems into small stanzas across the top of the page to represent cloud formations? If you write about a skyscraper, can the poem look like a building and the white space look like skyline?

Poems that look like their subjects are called concrete poems. You can also write a concrete poem about other things such as a tree, a flower, a vase, a perfume bottle, a missile, a house, etc. Form the words of the poem on the page to look like the poem.

Exercise 2: A Poem The Size Of A Flea

Consider writing a very small poem about a very small object (such as a stone or a shell) or to take a very large object (a planet, a building, a house) and position it on the page in an unlikely place (like the lower right corner). Play around with the many choices you have with space by trying new ways to see your poem on the page.

Exercise 3: Shapes On A Page

Write a poem that considers a specific space in a home or building such as an office, desk, file cabinet, kitchen etc.

For example, if you're looking at an office, what do you notice? Do you need two staplers? Three rulers? Five dictionaries? Or six years of *The New Yorker* you haven't read? What about the papers from first grade? First love letter? Your first mortgage or divorce papers? Maybe you now believe your filing cabinet is a stand-up coffin.

Arrange the images of items you have chosen around the page to mirror the set-up of the space. Try to step away from how you always write poems, and allow the white space and the images to tell a story about that location.

Exercise 4: Just Breathe

More and more studies focus on the benefits of meditation. By meditating, we create "blank space" in our minds. Doctors suggest that puzzles, exercise, and meditation help people with brain injuries. The same is true for people who don't suffer from the effects of brain injuries. According to Mayo Clinic staff, meditation helps people build self-awareness and reduce negative emotions. One of the results, of course, is obvious: Quiet. We clear away the information overload that bangs at our minds every day and we focus. We want to be in that same space when we're writing. True, we want our imagination working 100%. We want to snag new ideas out of our subconscious. We want to be ready for the muse to come calling. But to do that we need to be present. Focused.

If you practice meditation, continue with whatever technique you use. There are many types of meditations, including guided, mantra, tai chi, transcendental, and yoga. If you are new to meditation, play it simple: Focus on your breathing and let everything else go.

If you don't have a meditation practice, for this exercise set a timer for 5 – 10 minutes, close your eyes, and focus on each breath you take. When a thought comes into your mind, imagine it in a bubble and floating away.

Once the timer goes off, immediately write a poem about one of the thoughts that came into your mind. As you write, consider the white space of the page and allow the poem to have more white space than words.

Exercise 5: Give Me Some Space

Take a poem you have already written and revise it by adding more white space to it. You can add space between words, lines, and stanzas. Once you are done, revise the same poem by moving words around, using more/less white space to see what you like best.

Poems To Inspire Your Work:

WE SPEAK OF WATER
   for Ilya Kaminsky

       and he raises

a glass   gestures

       with his free

            arm as if a water

       fowl is being

raised from within

(this is California, Southern)

—*You must have water*—

I am filled   I might tell

        him of the many

nights I have been dreaming

of Fabergé   how dancing

on eggs   in dream   is more

        like floating

how floating   is more

        like eating

        down

plucking   feather after   (invisible)

   feather   from one's throat

      irritates   the esophagus

The truth is

        I have been   speaking

    to another

who knows   about   double

osmosis   He tells me   what

    becomes   of fluids

before preserving   before   the viewing

    about water   after water

where drains   in morgues

        empty

   how   California   is

      the great recycler

The truth is   I don't know this   yet

    The truth is   I am not

      thirsty   The truth is

always

    like separating egg   from apricot

by Natasha Kochicheril Moni

ꝏ

GUDDU'S GIRL
   After Maaza Mengiste

daddy   the command came out your mouth   you told them
to pick me up   to pull me out   the revolution   against you
of course they tore me   shred by shred I said your name
every night   I called on you   father   I thought
you could be some good even if it was your men
who bit my nipples with a car jump   who seared my skin
who ripped the very flesh of your flesh from my bones

by Hiwot Adilow

FUNERAL PERFUME

                Because
           the scent of death
          is absent, we smell
           the chemicals
        from the drycleaners
            on his suit,
             the hint
            of makeup
           on his face.
Because white Casablanca lilies
can overwhelm a family, we set them
outside on the steps of a too-cold day.
Because Aunt Mattie insists on smoking.
Because Uncle Lou wears Old Spice
and his suit lingers with mothballs.
Because there are scientists who say
a certain smell can return us to a day
faster than anything else, so knowing
that fear, that we will have to relive this
again in our memory, we open the doors
    wide, so wide we hear the traffic
outside during the eulogy. Because
    she didn't want to remember,
she wore a perfume she disliked
to the funeral, a sample from
     a department store,
a brand the saleslady told her
    they were discontinuing.

by Kelli Russell Agodon

Chapter 8: Color Outside the Lines

Remember shopping for Crayola crayons before school began—their sharp points and the smell of wax and something more—color? You could hold a stick of color in your hands and make anything come true.

Compare the feelings you get from the following two definitions:

Colorless: pale, neutral, dull.
Colorful: vivid, picturesque, bright.

Now, go deeper with some of the verbs associated with colors: infuse, chalk, daub, gild, lacquer, glaze, tint, stain, dye, embellish, adorn, imbue, rouge, etc.

The first box of Crayola Crayons was introduced by Binney & Smith, sold for five cents in 1903, and included brown, red, orange, yellow, green, blue, violet, and black.

Now Crayola Crayons has a box of 120 colors, which include: blue, black, brown, green, orange, red, violet (purple), yellow, carnation pink, blue green, blue violet, red orange, red violet, white, yellow green, yellow orange, apricot, cerulean, dandelion, gray, green yellow, indigo, scarlet, violet red, cadet blue, chestnut, melon, peach, sky blue, tan, timberwolf, wisteria, burnt sienna, cornflower, goldenrod, granny smith apple, lavender, macaroni and cheese, mahogany, mauvelous, olive green, purple mountains' majesty, raw sienna, salmon, sea green, sepia, spring green, tumbleweed asparagus, bittersweet, brick red, burnt orange, forest green, magenta, periwinkle, orchid, pacific blue, plum, robin's egg blue, spring green, silver, tickle me pink, turquoise blue, wild strawberry, atomic tangerine, cerise, copper, denim, electric lime, fuchsia, hot magenta, inchworm, jazzberry jam, jungle green, laser lemon, mango tango, maroon, midnight blue, navy blue, neon carrot, outrageous orange, pine green, purple pizzazz, radical red, razzle dazzle rose, razzmatazz, royal purple, screamin' green, shamrock, shocking pink, sunglow, tropical rain forest, unmellow yellow, vivid tangerine, wild watermelon, wild blue yonder, almond, antique brass, aquamarine, beaver, banana mania, blue bell, blushcaribbean green, canary, cotton candy, desert sand, eggplant, fern, fuzzy wuzzy, manatee, mountain meadow, outer space, piggy pink, pink flamingo, pink sherbet, purple heart, shadow, sunset orange, vivid violet.

Add to those colors the following definitions and objects from the 1971 *Webster's New World Thesaurus*:

brown: chestnut, cinnamon, coffee, dun, liver-colored, mahogany
red: bittersweet, Congo red, crimson, fuchsin, russet, rust, saffron, vermillion
orange: bergamot, coral, ocherous, salmon
yellow: alizarin yellow, golden, lemon, old ivory
green: emerald, jade, lime, sea-green, vert
blue: azure, indigo, Prussian, sapphire, sapphirine, turquoise
violet: lavender, mauve, round-leaved, purplish
black: coal, dusky, ebony, jet black, raven-hued
white: ashen, bleached, chalky, frosted, ivory, milky, pearly

Exercise 1: Goodbye My Maize

In 1990, eight Crayola colors disappeared out of the limelight to land in Crayola's Hall of Fame. Crayola replaced these colors: maize, raw umber, blue-gray, lemon yellow, green blue, orange yellow, orange red, and violet blue with the following new colors: dandelion, wild strawberry, vivid tangerine, fuchsia, teal blue, royal purple, jungle green, and cerulean.

Write a poem to one of these retired or new colors. Maybe title it "Ode to Vivid Tangerine" or "For the Love of Royal Purple." Or chose another color from the list above and write a poem in celebration of it. Try to include many images of that color in your poem. For example, if you choose "lemon yellow," you might include the words sun, caution sign, leaves in autumn, banana, taxi cab, etc.

Exercise 2: My Love is Like a Red, Red, Red, Red Rose

Write a poem that uses one color repeatedly throughout. You can choose your color from the large list of Crayola colors, or maybe you just want to go old school with primary colors like blue, red, or yellow.

Once you've chosen a color, repeat it as many times as you can in your poem. If you choose the color blue, your images may include: *blue dress, blue sorrow, blue cloud on a blue day.* Allow the sounds of the color to move you forward in the poem. Don't worry if your poem is not making sense, but let the sounds and repetition move you forward. You can revise your poem later.

Here are some possibilities for titling the poem:

"What _____ (blue, green, indigo, etc.) Had to Say"
"Listening To _____" (cinnamon, sunflower, haystack, etc.)

"In the Season of _____" (red, yellow, blue, etc.)

Exercise 3: Brown Rock, White Paper, Silver Scissors

Write a poem with images that are a specific color. Maybe you have a black cat sitting on a blue blanket or a yellow dog running beneath an indigo sky. The poem does not need to be complicated, but can explore a simple scene (think of William Carlos Williams' "The Red Wheelbarrow"). To begin the poem, start with an image and go from there.

Poems To Inspire Your Work:

THE WHITE ROPE

A white rope
leads from the house
to the door of the red barn.
During blizzards
a gloved hand slides along the rope.
Inside the house
three generations of one family.
Inside the barn
the animals
we depend on.

by Netter Hansen

೫

REMNANTS

Under the arbor
smothered in pale pink-petaled roses
a gangway leads down the dock
life rings mounted
crab pots splintered
cracked flower boxes filled with

hostas and hollyhock.
A child's purple scooter
rests against a blue wall.

by Susan Jostrom

☞

GREEN WILLOW WIFE

I begged you not to take me far
from home, I was so young, my black hair
uncut and unbound, loose over your hands, my feet bare
while I poured you warm sake by the fire.

We roamed villages, me in the foamy green clothing
you bought for my thin legs and shoulders.
I'm so tired, I'll die, I told you. I lay down
on the wet grass beside the river. How I loved you,
my husband, do not forget your green willow.
In the morning, all that was left of me
was my green silk scarf and skirt
and a sheaf of green willow leaves.

When you went back to my village, grieving,
the three willow trees in front of my house
cut down, and the house itself decayed,
my parents missing... Poor husband,

you should have known the green willow
could not stray far. Let me lie down on the grass.
Let the rain fall on the stumps of my soul.
Remember the green willow,

who gave you her young limbs,
with whom you lay on white wooden mats.

by Jeannine Hall Gailey

Chapter 9: My Body, My Poem

Some people listen to their bodies more than others. Some of us accept them; others wish for bodies that are better, thinner, healthier, or more muscled. Poems wait to be written about our bodies and its experiences–snappy, saucy, funny, and sad poems.

Exercise 1: To My Dear Hips

Pick a body part you're the least fond of or you wish was bigger or smaller, more lovely, less crooked, or more sleek or curly. Write a letter to that body part by hand, using a pen or pencil. Be specific but don't overthink. Write for five minutes without pausing, not worrying about grammar, punctuation, or spelling. For example:

Dear Feet,
I can't curse you because you carry me, but you ache every day in spite of creams and soak baths. I close off the sight of you with your bunions and flaky skin in my shoes, but you cramp and you smell like my grandmother's...

Now, have that body part write back to you. Again, use pen or pencil. Be specific, and don't overthink. Write for five minutes without pausing and don't worry about grammar, punctuation, or spelling. For example:

Dear (your name here),
You're right. I carry you. I've carried you except for the time you sprained your ankle, but all I ever hear from you poisons my resolves to be happy feet. Have you never counted the steps I take each day...

Note the tone of your two letters and choose the best words and lines from what you've written and write a poem.

Exercise 2: I Sing The Body...

Consider the following facts about the human body:

- —We all have a unique tongue print
- —Our skin is the largest organ of our body
- —Our body has an average of 37.2 trillion cells
- —Our bones are as strong as granite
- —We have approximately 60,000 miles of blood vessels

—We wake up taller than when we went to sleep
—We use 17 muscles to smile and 43 to frown
—In one day blood travels 12,000 miles around our body
—We are mostly fungi and bacteria
—We shed approximately 1.5 pounds of skin a year

Write a poem about one or two facts from the above list, and how that fact(s) affects your understanding of your body. *Really? I have 37.2 trillion cells? How many bus stops, train stations, and bars are situated along my 60,000 miles of blood vessels? Maybe I'm giving my face a workout today by frowning at my significant other.* Your poem can be humorous or serious or perhaps you want to celebrate this amazing human body we all find ourselves housed in. In 1855 Walt Whitman published "I Sing the Body Electric." He was one of the first poets to specifically write about the human body and sexuality. Here is an excerpt from his poem:

Food, drink, pulse, digestion, sweat, sleep, walking, swimming,
Poise on the hips, leaping, reclining, embracing, arm-curving and tightening,
The continual changes of the flex of the mouth, and around the eyes,
The skin, the sunburnt shade, freckles, hair,
The curious sympathy one feels when feeling with the hand the naked meat
    of the body,
The circling rivers the breath, and breathing it in and out,
The beauty of the waist, and thence of the hips, and thence downward toward
    the knees,
The thin red jellies within you or within me, the bones and the marrow in the
    bones,
The exquisite realization of health...

Exercise 3: Cry Me A River

Tears are made differently by our bodies depending on the reason that we are crying. The tears we shed in grief are not the same as the tears of happiness. Neither are they the same tears we shed when we peel onions or have an allergy attack. Write a poem that makes you cry and feel emotional as you compose it. Maybe the tears are those of loss and grief, or perhaps the tears flow from a tremendous sense of thankfulness and gratitude. Try not to edit your writing, but allow words and images to flow unimpeded—this will help you to stay emotionally engaged with your subject matter.

Poems To Inspire Your Work:

GIRL

Open your right palm, note the smallest finger,
more exactly, the bone between the two joints,
and only the delicate front of that bone.
This portion is what remains of a third species
of hominid,
    an ancient cousin,
        living 40,000 years ago.

But even the fragment is now gone, scientiests
recently grinding up this bit to decode its DNA
proving the species new, its presence persisting
today in the mitochondria
    yet coloring
        our twist of genetics.

The bone's reduction reveals this being was female
with dark skin and hair. Her age was five years old,
her cartilage newly hardened to bone. She died
by herself,
    gathering food,
        lost in color, warmth, reflection,

involved as is the girl holding a plastic bowl,
picking raspberries in my garden out back.

by Ann Spiers

ꟹ

BODY POLITIC

Praise our scars—
the small gashes
and the long,
serpentine tracks

that make up
our unbeauty.
Scar, from the
Greek word eschara,
meaning place of fire.
This is the body's politic,
reminding us that
the past existed.
Inside, what is tender
is retreaded by our living,
by wounds in the sidewalks
of dry skin. Never once
do we question
the sinkholes our bodies
drive into and repair
day after day.
No one but our
doctor or lover
can read the map
to our hurting.

by January Gill O'Neil

☯

HOW TO HOLD A HEART
~Instructions to a cardiac surgeon.

Weighing ten ounces, the heart feels unexpectedly heavy.
An organ you could palm, but don't, as it is slippery
with blood and the surprise of pulsing. Pulsing
even later, as you lay it in a stainless-steel basin.

So best to use two hands.
Hook your cupped palms together,
linking the pinkies, to create a basket
cradling the dislodged and beating heart.

What will you do as it bleeds out?
Turn your back, ready the not-so-new new heart
as the nurse whisks away the old to the fire.
Or do you blink your eyes closed
long enough for inhale, exhale.

Long enough to consider him as your hand unfurls,
fingers graze his shoulder, assess his condition:
neither dead nor alive, heartless,
free from the expectation to love,
to be that perfect someone, that one and only.

by Heidi Seaborn

Chapter 10: Connotations

What does the word *red* mean? Jot down your immediate answer. (Note: there is no wrong answer. Red is associated with fire, garnet, rose, anger, blood, stoplights, and more. To you, it could mean love, but to someone else it could mean hate.)

According to *Merriam-Webster's Collegiate Dictionary Eleventh Edition*, red is defined as "of the color red…having red as a distinguishing color." Actually, there are two inches of definition, including the fact that red means "reduce; reduction."

In *The Merriam Webster Dictionary 50th Anniversary Edition*, red means: "of the color red…endorsing radical social or political change esp. by force." There is no mention of "reduce; reduction."

The above dictionary definitions are termed *denotation*. They carry a specific meaning; they denote or designate.

Connotation, on the other hand, means the implication of words that carry emotional or cultural meanings. Sometimes those are positive, sometimes negative. The word *politician* might set some people's teeth on edge while the word *statesman* paints a different picture. The word *emotional* can mean both *impulsive* and *spontaneous*. *Impulsive* implies acting without much thought, the latter being able to think on one's feet.

Interesting that the *Webster's New Collegiate Dictionary* from 1977 (hardback) included the following for the word *connotation*: "the signification of something" and then gave the example "that abuse of logic which consists in moving counters about as if they were known entities with a fixed connotation." The 1974 *Merriam-Webster Dictionary* (soft cover) defined *connotation* as "meaning in addition to or apart from the thing explicitly named or described by a word."

Thus, one dictionary is not exactly the same as other dictionaries. And each person's connotative definition of a word is not the same as every other person's association with a word. We bring our experiences, memories, and ideas to words, which means that the word *red* can bring to one person's mind an image that is different from what another person "sees" when that word is used.

In the following exercises, trust your own connotations of words. As a poet, your feelings and associations with words can bring new layers and levels to your poetry.

Exercise 1: Tiptoe Through The Tulips

Flowers: we give them to show love or friendship. We surround ourselves with them at weddings and at funerals. Annuals die at the end of their growing season (usually summer or fall), whereas perennials come up again and again. Some flowers, such as crocus, daffodils, and grape hyacinths, come up even with snow on the ground. Flowers bloom beautifully, then die, sometimes within days. They remind us, as Janis Joplin sang: "We may not be here tomorrow... Get it while you can."

Write a poem about a flower that evokes within you a certain feeling. For example, some people love lilies at Easter because they remind them of spring and new life. But a widow, who received several pots of lilies after her husband died, may associate lilies with mourning, funerals, and loss.

Exercise 2: A Poem Of Associations

Choose a word or object from the following list, and write down everything that comes to mind regarding that word:

>   bat
>   bed
>   cabbage
>   dark
>   garbage
>   icicle
>   knife
>   nightmare
>   pillar
>   salt
>   shore
>   orange
>   white

Once you have made your list, write a poem using only your associations for that word, not its definition. For example, if you chose "nightmare," your words and images might include: *dreamlike, on Elm Street, Freddy Krueger, late for class, midnight, witching hour, stuck in a tunnel underground, teeth falling out, raven, crow, darkness, before Christmas, Tim Burton.* And here are some possible associations for the word orange: *eye, moon, pumpkin, seed, circle, juice, skin, crate.*

Write a poem using the words and associations you came up with. You may want to use either something about the word, or the word itself in your title—for example, if you chose "nightmare," your poem could be titled "The Meaning of Nightmare" or "The Meaning of Sleep," etc.

Poems To Inspire Your Work:

ROSE OF JERICHO

I'm not sure about this gift. This tangle
of dried roots curled into a fist. This gnarl

I've let sit for weeks beside the toaster
and cookbooks on a bed of speckled granite.

What am I waiting for? Online I find
Rose of Jericho spells and rituals for safe birth,

well-being, warding off the evil eye.
At first I thought I'd buy some white stones,

a porcelain bowl. But I didn't and I didn't.
I don't believe in omens. This still fist

of possibility all wrapped up in itself.
There it sat through the holidays, into the New Year.

Through all the days I've been gone. Dormant.
But today, in an inch of water,

out of curiosity, I awakened
the soul of Jericho. Limb by limb it unfolded

and turned moss green. It reminded me
of the northwest, its lush undergrowth,

how twice despite the leaden clouds,
the rain, I found happiness there.

From tumbleweed to lush fern flower,
reversible, repeatable. And what am I

to make of this? Me, this woman who doesn't
believe. Doesn't take anything on faith. I won't

let it rot. I'll monitor the water level. Keep the mold
at bay. I tend things, but I do not pray.

by Cindy Veach

EVERY SUNDAY AT THE GROCERY STORE

your ex-wife buys a bouquet,
unaware of my stare as I stock
shelves. You may have failed

to tell her of me. I've never
grasped what to do when flowers
start wilting—to press them,

compost them, throw them
in the sea. She knows,
her skirt an extravagant

bloom in the gust of a closing door.

by Lauren Davis

MAY FLOWERS

In early May in sunlight,
concrete homes nestle in wisteria clusters
on the hills, their colors dappled
as the brows of old women, their windows
glinting gold teeth in mouths full of story.

A rainy winter is no promise of comfort,
no respite in valleys of thirst.
A rainy winter is the bone-chill of walls
dampening, cold
sweat of cinder blocks.

This is the part of town where the houses still
lean into one another shouldering sorrows,
metal gates tarnished amber as vinegar
collecting daylight in jars on the windowsill.

This is the part of town where turquoise sky
hemmed with satellite dishes and
crowded with minarets threading
prayers in its seams
awakens again to
May on the other side of waiting.

Beyond the dreamscape of marble-floored
villas and manicured drought along the border,
the earth drinks every ounce
of rain, sends red poppies,
wild-thyme refugees
drifting across hillsides.
Beyond the dreamscape the barbed wire
curls and sinews,
languid on the low walls.

This is the part of town where girls
buy loaves of thin bread wrapped in yesterday's news
and boys chase stray cats down numberless streets.

This is the part of town where
there are always children outside,
their voices an echo of villages lost,
their kites heralding the sunset,
May flowers in the East Amman sky.

by Lena Khalaf Tuffaha

Chapter 11: The Trickster Coyote

Stanley Kunitz said, "A poet needs to keep his wilderness inside him." Let's start with the coyote. In the past, the coyote was personified as both cunning and good—a trickster/shaman. Before books, the telegraph, radio, and the internet, people told stories. The NIMIIPUU (Nez Perce) in Idaho, as did many Native Americans and peoples with an oral tradition, often explained the world with animal stories. Coyote stories in the NIMIIPUU world explained the inexplicable—how humans got fire, how the Seven Devils Mountains came to be, and how humans were born.

In their stories, beaver stole fire from the pines. The Seven Devils Mountains were originally seven giant brothers that ate children. With Fox's help, Coyote dug pits that the giants fell into. Coyote changed the brothers into the seven high peaks. They stand in a semicircle on the Idaho side of what is considered to be the deepest canyon on the North American continent—Hell's Canyon of the Snake River.

Coyote can be found in many stories and myths ranging from "Coyote and Hummingbird" and "Coyote and the Moon" to "Coyote Visits the Land of the Dead" and "How Coyote's Manhood Becomes a Dam." Of course, coyote is also credited with creating the earth and human beings—"Coyote Creates the Earth" and "Coyote Creates Human Beings."

Rex Lee Jim, a Diné (Navajo) poet, has written a number of poems about coyote. His poem written in both Diné Bizaad (the Navajo language) and English, "Na'azheeh / Hunting," begins "Click / I stole your breathing..."

I have respect and a particular fondness for coyotes, which began when I moved into my current home. A protected area known as Bingaman Pond starts on the other side of my fence. This 17-acre property includes a wetland that was dammed for cranberry production years ago. Now the wetland houses snakes, woodpeckers, an owl, trilliums, ferns, cottonwood trees, firs, pine, and at least one coyote. Before my neighborhood was built up, I saw a coyote pup on one of the new house sites; I also saw an adult just over my fence. The adult definitely looked like a trickster. I wouldn't want to face one alone, but I love his/her howl. When his/her barks or yelps or howls startle me awake at 4 a.m., setting goosebumps on my neck and arms, I am reminded of the wildness we don't often think about in this world of iPhones, freeways, and fast food drive-thrus. Coyote howls raise not only anxiety and fear in me but a sense of wonder, a memory I didn't know I remembered. It's the real "wilderness" inside me that Kunitz said a poet "needs to keep."

Exercise 1: Why Coyote Created Lightning

Write a list of words that have to do with the *wild* or *wildness*. For example:

woods, caves, slugs, leaves, trails, howls, snapping twigs, tunnels, lightning, lush, dense, weedy, primeval—whatever word associations come to you.

Next, write a list of words for *wile*, such as deceit, trick, deception, lie, cheat, bluff, etc.

Finally, write a list of words for *shaman*, such as healer, potion, doctor, renew, cure, drug, restore, ointment, etc.

Now, write a poem that incorporates some of the words from your lists above and explains how something natural was created or how some human condition came to be. You can use a coyote as your main subject, or you can choose another animal that you feel a particular connection with. How was the first storm made? By a swarm of fireflies or an angry coyote or mating seagulls? Don't worry about scientific explanations and facts, but allow your imaginings to create stories of how certain things in our world came to be. Perhaps each act of creation contained elements of both *wile* and *shamanism*. Maybe a salmon created waterfalls or maybe elephants made the first lake. Which animal put tassels on corn and shook the leaves each autumn off the trees? Which animal decided that pumpkins should grow on vines on the ground? Did a Maine Coon cat spark the idea for quantum theory? Did owls orchestrate how people learned which mushrooms were safe to pick, or did dolphins decide that people need two hands with five digits?

Exercise 2: Crows And Ravens

In keeping with the theme of animals and the wilderness within us, write a poem where the "character" is a crow or raven, both of which have a lot to say. They are loud and smart, among the smartest animals on the planet. They can imitate many sounds, including meowing cats and barking dogs. They can recognize a human's face.

Here are some interesting notes about crows:

    —Live all over the world, except in Antarctica
    —They are scavengers and will eat anything
    —They are social and live in large groups
    —A group of these birds is called a "murder of crows"

—Crows mate for life

In his poem, "Crow Blacker Than Ever" from his book *Crow: from the Life and Songs of the Crow*, Ted Hughes writes:

> Things looked like falling apart.
> But Crow Crow
>   Crow nailed them together–

Here are some notes about ravens:

> —Similar species as the crow but larger
> —Ravens soar more than crows
> —Ravens follow their predators
> —In case of short supply, ravens hide and stockpile food

Sherwin Bitsui writes in "The Skyline of a Missing Tooth":

> A raven's rib ripped from the electric socket
>   heats the palm
> its rusted core bound by the apple's shaven hide.

As you compose your crow/raven poem, think about their intriguing characteristics and your personal associations with these birds. Do you love them? Fear them? Find them irritating? What might a crow/raven be responsible for creating in the mythological realm—the game of poker, quarrels between lovers, the dark sky on a moonless night, bittersweet chocolate, sore scratchy throats? You can also simply write about a direct experience you have had with a crow/raven.

Poems To Inspire Your Work:

COYOTES

All night, those blue-throated howls—
parentheses opening over
barbed-wire fields. Pure frequency. Broken spirals—
Even new-moved from the city, I knew
they called to no moon. Like our neighbor
in Fort Worth, dancing all night in the street, raw-
singing and gin-spun, had called to no one

to save her. She terrified me: made me feel
my own bare feet on asphalt, the open turn
of a waltz into no arms. My mother drove
broken-glass-slowly, closed windows—
as if honeysuckle bees nested in that woman's
body's vines. *She has children.* (I never saw them.)
Sad life. But her songs were wilder
than sadness—a black oak's branches bent
only by nature, up. Bright Arkansas mornings,
we'd see fur tufted on fence posts, scat
in the grass by the shallow pond—droppings
of creatures beyond us. Safest and best:
the blue heron that floated for days—rare
as blown glass—in the pasture. We felt blessed
til it left us. We picked Queen Anne's Lace:
wild weed we called flowers. We did not howl.
We arranged the land inside our vases.

by Alexandra Teague

☙

AT THE ALTAR OF STAYING

A coyote in the road
straddling double yellow lines *no-*

passing flame-blue flickers
against the body's horizon

My mother watches
my small children sleeping

early I drive where sky quilts
mountains black

birds twinning
distance against my mother's face

lines in the road
trash I must resist

peeling roadside
& feeding

at the wick
another prayer

Henna girl you are not the coyote
skirting the edge

feeding fear's belly
ten cuidado ama

the animal in the center is wild
& sweetness

you're tough as tar

by Jennifer Givhan

୪ଠ

CANDLING

Say that it bloomed, put down roots, lodged

like an egg in a nest, snow in a cleft, wedged
for a winter's nap, say it

turned three times round, curled up
with its nose toward the door.

Say myometrium. Say wand. Say gel,
neoplasm, adenoma. Say benign.

Benign.

Put a light bulb behind it and watch it
tumesce.

Say the raven is growing
a new planet in your body.

Should the nascent body bloom, say
is this the beak, that the beginning of legs.

by Jenifer Browne Lawrence

Chapter 12: Writing Into Our Fears

We all have met fear in our lives. It's a great motivator with two possibilities: flight or fight. Fear comes with many names: fear of success, fear of failure, fear of closed spaces, fear of open spaces, fear of loud noises, fear of spiders, dogs, drowning, or heights, just to name a few.

Think about any fears you might currently have, as well as any fears you have overcome.

Exercise 1: It Tastes Like Brussels Sprouts

Choose one of your fears, then answer the following questions (be as creative and inventive as you can):

—What is its shape?
—What sound does your fear make?
—What does that fear taste like in your mouth?
—Where does that fear go when you aren't thinking about it?
—Where do you want it to go?
—What do you tell your fear? "Get lost." "Have a life somewhere else." Or "I've buried you under the big rock at Needle Pass. There were no witnesses."
—What does fear tell you?

Write a poem about fear using your answers to the above questions. It might be relieving to get that fear out on the page where you and your readers can see it and react to it.

Sometimes fear is so personal it's hard to write about. If you are having difficulty writing about your fear in the first person ("I"), try writing the poem from third person (he/she/they) in which you are observing yourself or the speaker struggling with this fear.

Consider using one of the following as an opening line, "When I saw fear, it said. . ." or "When fear arrived, it resembled a. . ."

Exercise 2: Bake An Anxiety Cake

Write a recipe poem using fear as your inspiration. Recipes use active verbs and are not filled with rhetoric. They're didactic, to the point, with specific instructions:

> Sauté 3 cloves garlic and 1 onion chopped in 1 tsp. of olive oil
> Add 1 pound ground beef
> Add 1 cup white rice
> Add 1 can of diced tomatoes
> Simmer for 10 minutes

Write a recipe poem about a specific fear in the form of a recipe. Think about what you're going to do to get rid of this fear, what you would add, subtract, or mix in. You can use a recipe card format, but go outside the box in terms of ideas, phrases, etc.

For the title of your poem, look up the clinical name for your fear. If you're afraid of open spaces, your poem could be called "Recipe to Reverse Agoraphobia" and include lines like:

> Cut out pictures of open fields and parks from magazines and flyers.
> Paste them in a scrapbook.
> Practice keeping the draperies open for a half hour each day.
> Ask my friend Alice to go with me to the park.
> Wear sunglasses.
> Pretend I'm someone else, maybe a dog.
> Dogs love open spaces.
> Repeat several times a day: Martians don't like open spaces, but I do.

Consider writing several recipe poems using different fears as your inspiration.

Poems To Inspire Your Work:

DRIVING AT NIGHT TOWARDS THE HOOD CANAL

Even when I am not
speeding I get stopped
for speeding and there

is no room for a question
to a cop positioning his
shooting stance outside

my rolled down window
in the dangerous wash
of red and blue lights

the Dirty Harry Dixie
a murder soundtrack
we both know is playing

and there is no protest from
or protection for me there is
the skim of this moment

that thin layer of skin
covering the whole situation
there is only the space

of a breath between
what should happen
and what could happen

by Gary Copeland Lilley

℘

AGORAPHOBIA: AFTER CAMP

She pulls the front door shut
and turns the key until it's firm.
She pulls the blanket close and
stands behind the curtains,
turns the radio low, and watches
the gauzy world sway and
pass her window.

Children play across the street;
they hit a ball before the cars
arrive. When the ball hits
her window, it rattles like a
lost pigeon flying unseeing

into a mirror, like a neighbor
wondering when and if
anyone is ever home.

When someone rings the bell
she sits in silence until
the steps retreat. The shades
are pulled; even at dusk
she keeps the room unlit
so no one passing by
will know how slowly
a day can pass.

Call screening keeps the voices
from the outside world
from entering past her phone.
She has enough of visitors
who won't remove themselves.
Fingers in her ears will not
remove their cries.

Does she savor every
moment and every breath
of every second of every day?
Even in the dusk of living
the wrinkles accrue like taxes,
her hair a thinning testament
to that life islanded against the world.

by Lonny Kaneko

☙

FROM A ROMAN WINDOW

She stares from an open casement across the well
between our buildings, seeming unaware
her nightgown has outgrown her, falls
from a wizened shoulder. Her eyes seem fearful,
her soft half-opened mouth

like the Magdalene of Donatello –
saved from devils, a look of "pity and ruth,"
her riven body painted wood and tow.

She drops her gaze, sees us, flushes.
What devils were they? Flesh becoming word,
word forgetting that it had been flesh?
Half turning away, she adjusts her wayward gown.
Who isn't fearful in a dying world?
(She nods as though she'd like to paint the town.)

by Robert McNamara

Chapter 13: Write Your Townscape

Take some time and reflect on the town/city/countryside where you grew up. If your family moved frequently, pick the place that most feels like "home" to you or the place where the most significant events in your life occurred as you were growing up. Visualize the surrounding town/city/countryside; next visualize your specific neighborhood; and now visualize your house or apartment building. What color was your home? What sort of architecture or style? Was there a yard? Trees? Play equipment or patio furniture? Was it on a quiet street or a busy avenue?

On a piece of paper sketch where you grew up by creating your own map of memories—draw and label your house, your school(s), the grocery store, the library, etc. If you have the ability to go online, visit Google maps and look at where you grew up on the "satellite view"—can you see your house or apartment building? The yard? Drop to street level and actually "stand" on the street in front of the living space where you grew up. Note what is the same and what is different, and note how you feel.

Take an imaginary walk around the town/city/countryside where you grew up. Who lived next door to you? Can you remember their specific names? Imagine walking/being driven to your school. Pick a year from your childhood and think about how everything would appear—clothing styles, car models, what movies might be playing at the local theater—1959? 1979? 1999? What did you know in that year about your neighborhood, about your family, about yourself? Immerse yourself in these memories.

How far do you currently live from where you grew up? Are you relatively close by or do you now live across the country or in a different country altogether? Would you want to return to your old neighborhood and live there again? Why or why not?

Exercise 1: An Afternoon On Walnut Street, 1980

Write a poem about your town/city/countryside or the neighborhood or the street you lived on. Focus on what people did there, the names of streets, stores, schools, restaurants, and parks. Take the poem's reader on a walk through that place, and allow them to experience sounds, smells, the pace of life, the joy and/or difficulty. Use your responses to the questions posed in the introduction to this exercise—maybe pick a certain year to write about or a specific experience that happened in a store, park, or backyard.

Exercise 2: This Did Not Happen

Write a poem about what you wish had <u>not</u> happened in your town/city or countryside. This could be something very personal or something involving many people. For example:

> —You didn't have a huge fight with your best friend after the football game.
> —Your parents did not divorce during your sophomore year of high school.
> —Your neighbor's house did not burn to the ground in the middle of the night.
> —The town's drinking water was not contaminated with lead.

Take your reader to that time and place. Be specific; give as many details as possible, including detailed descriptions about the incident and the people involved.

Exercise 3: This Did Happen

Write a poem about what you wish had happened in your town/city/or countryside. As in the exercise above, this experience can be very personal or something involving many people. For example:

> —You won the lottery and paid off the mortgage on your parent's house just before the bank foreclosed on it.
> —The boy/girl you had a crush on in high school also had a crush on you.
> —Your town received federal grant money to clean up the toxic dumping site that slowly poisoned the river.
> —Your neighbor with five children was found innocent and did not spend ten years in prison.

As in Exercise 2, give as much detail as possible to put your reader in this place in a specific period of time.

Poems To Inspire Your Work:

CAPE DISAPPOINTMENT

A day like this when Lewis and Clark reached the Pacific,
no more basalt cliffs to scale, swollen rivers to ford,

just shore pines hunched in wind, rain-sopped moss
and beyond, long curls of sea unscrolling.

I imagine them peeling off sweaty buckskin, dashing into the surf,
Seaman between them, the Corps lined up on shore,

maybe mustering a jig. But it was November, the storm raged
all week. They hunkered down at the Dismal Nitch, listened

to the sea's incessant grumble, tent restive in wind, riven with rain,
debated where to winter. The Pacific at last, but not the end

of the journey. The worst winter ahead, then the long trek back
across the continent. Here's what I want to know:

For how long was the Pacific the shimmering ring
they could at last reach out and grab, before they turned

their backs on her bright face, settled into the dripping moss,
dried their soaked boots by the fire, ocean now a mumbling counterpoint?

The destination glittering ahead, but kindling to gather,
a reluctant fire to fan, that irritating sliver in the thumb.

A disappointment, Clark wrote in his journal. Was it
just all those miles to reel back to their lives?

I rise early, pack the car, no time for one more walk
along the sea. Disappointment trails me like an orphan,

fetching up with all the long-stuffed grievances:
that ill-fitting coat in seventh grade, turned bottle of wine,

even the man you love who lets you down
in ways too petty to name. All the way home,

in the rearview mirror, she's there, still,
her gold ring shimmering.

by Holly Hughes

☙

AS WE FLOAT TOWARDS THE PACIFIC, THE CLOUDS APPEAR HEARTSHAPED

Now that we've moved to Seattle,
we will buy copper river salmon steaks
on sale at Safeway for $4.95 a pound,
pink and thick, eat them
Wednesdays when the sun shines.

We will scrub the spider webs of North Dakota
from our bumpers, the dead bugs of Montana
off our grill.

You fold the cardboard I carry
to the curb. I cut grass.
You bake bread.
We fix the broken freezer.

You are my paper marigolds, my Marco, my Polo,
my new blue swings.
You are river stones in the garden.

If this were the last day, still
where I would choose to be,
the ocean near our backs.

How will I remember you
in twenty years? With grapes in hand
you say, grapes in hand.

by Deborah Bacharach

UNION STATION

The clock face lifts
above December fog.
Two empty boxcars
rust in this deserted yard
where track winds intricate
as memory. Inside, oak benches
worn smooth by years
of hands and bodies pressed
like mounds of luggage
heaped on the marble floor,
where I traced patterns of grey veins
that ran between the Lucky butts
and coffee stains, the star
shaped locus point North

and South, *but we were going
East,* the last leg home
from Dallas to Wenatchee.
What we forget, the long years carry:
there's the candy store,
the dining room, the barber shop
and shoe shine stand, the ticket
booth, and just beyond the protest
of these metal doors,
rows of yellow cabs
and red caps bob beside the tilting
luggage racks. My mother's sharp heels
mark staccato grief. What remains
is silence: the acrid smell of diesel
dust buried in this yard.

by Julianne Seeman

Chapter 14: Po-Jack 101

The term "po-jack" refers to "hijacking" or borrowing aspects of a specific poem in the composition of your poem. When you practice "po-jacking" it is best to give credit to the poet, whose style is providing you with inspiration, in an epigraph or in an endnote. The goal of po-jacking is to be inspired by poems, not to plagiarize another poet's material, so please remember to give credit to your source of inspiration.

Exercise 1: Po-Jacking Basics

Choose two contemporary poems by two different poets whose work you find inspirational. To begin, analyze each poem by identifying and making notes on the following poetic elements:

—nouns and active verbs
—enjambments and end-stopped lines
—internal rhyme and alliteration, similes and metaphors
—passive verbs and adjectives
—rhythm
—stanzas, indenting, the use of numbers, white space, etc.
—format—is the poem a sonnet, villanelle, haiku, etc.

Dig into the meaning of each poem. What is the theme or message? How has the language conveyed that theme or message? Is the poet's voice informal and conversational? Is the poem's mood uplifting, sorrowful, angry, political, humorous, etc.?

Now list techniques that each poet has used. Do the poems

—make use of images?
—vary one-syllable and multi-syllabic words?
—end lines on a strong word or image; or use a strong words or images at the beginning of each line?
—use internal rhyme?
—use the title as integral to the meaning of the poem?
—use similes and metaphors?

Exercise 2: Po-Jacking Form And Structure

Choose one of the two poems and imitate it. Write your poem following its form, structure, and syllable count. Use an article for each article, a noun for each noun, etc. If possible, use the same number of syllables per word (such as armor for basin, tomorrow for yesterday). Use the same number of words per line, and follow the same pattern of stanzas.

For instance, if the poem's title is "Following the Professor," your poem might be titled "Translating a Janitor." If the first line is "He had this gait, like a hippo on land," your poem about the janitor might be "He stayed his shift, like a watchman on call."

Exercise 3: Po-Jacking Tone And Voice

For this exercise you will use the poem that you did not choose for Exercise 2. In your poem, copy this poem's tone and voice—is it angry, joyful, sad, analytical, humorous, insightful, dreamlike, regretful, scolding, etc.? Below are some examples of tone and voice that are different and distinct. Compare and contrast Mary Oliver with Ruth Stone:

Oliver begins her poem "Invitation" in her collection *Red Bird* with "Oh do you have time/to linger…" Stone begins her poem "Reading the Russians" in *In the Next Galaxy* with "Of course they are gloomy; / they drink a lot of vodka…"

Note the differences between Robert Pinsky's voice and Kwame Dawes's voice:

Pinsky begins the poem "In the Coma" with "My friend was in a coma, so I dove / Deep into his brain to word him back…" Dawes begins his poem "Lasta Mountains" from his collection *Wheels* with: "There among the rocks of Roha / the stone obeys the chisel and muscle…"

As you have probably noted, Oliver's tone is inviting whereas Stone's poem is more didactic. Pinsky's tone reflects his personal "I" unlike the omniscient voice of Dawes.

Identify the tone and voice of your chosen poem and copy it as you compose your own piece. Po-jack or borrow some of the words in the poem that convey the tone and voice. If the poem uses "I" as the speaker, do the same. If you are inspired by the theme or topic of the poem, choose a similar theme or topic to help you more closely imitate the voice and tone.

Poems To Inspire Your Work:

HOW TO VOTE LIKE A GIRL
   after Ada Limón

Ladies, believe me when I say the buttonhole
blooms possibility. Slip the round knob
in the threaded slot like you mean it,
like that mother-of-pearl is your inheritance.
Did you gather your acre of fabric
and sew like a mule, eight miles an hour,
seventy-seven cents on the dollar, the whole
god-damned day? Yes, there will be blood
in the selvage. Imagine yourself the heroine,
your hand wielding the awl, you the one
who makes the machine snarl.

by Elizabeth Austen
Inspired by "How To Triumph Like a Girl" by Ada Limón

℘

DEGREES OF WHITE IN WASHINGTON

You might have come here last Sunday on a whim,
the last good snow years ago.
You walked these streets laid out by the threatening ice
past cars that didn't make it, Jeeps that did, and
the tortured lot of local drivers who accelerated.
Prisoners now, not knowing what to do.

The principal supporting businesses are food and
hatred of this late winter storm
the mountain sent.
One open restaurant and bar can't
wipe out the boredom.
Traffic lights blink over
an empty dance floor built on black ice.
The snow rises two stacks above the deck,

a huge mountain in the parking lot
that refuses to finally dissolve.

Is this now your life?
The church bell is all announcement
but no one comes.
Towering oaks, good hooch, and wine
are all you have
until the whiteness ultimately relents.

The old woman next door,
twenty when her town was first built,
smiles at the memory of much worse.
Someday soon she'll go to sleep and not wake up.
You tell her no.
The car that brought you here still runs,
the fire in the grate still burns,
and the speechless green of spring waits its turn.

by Lea Galanter
Inspired by "Degrees of Gray in Philipsburg," by Richard Hugo

८०

INVITATION TO MR. W

Before the birds find their breakfast, before the clack of wooden
clogs advise me of my neighbor striding to her coop,
another woman turning on the sprinklers with a swoooshhhhhh.

Before I'm awake enough to call and question you again, before you
navigate with enigmatic answers and dead ends,
                    please come flying —

Over the Willamette that wends itself into town in a V,
over the Masonic cemetery replete with street lights, verses,
                    dear, please come flying —

In this summer of my 40th year, in this season of blackberries,
cherries, and inexplicably sweet pears, won't you
                    just come flying —

Forget your double life, your despairing heart, and other minor
irrelevancies. Come with your old blue van, come with your kayak
                    but do come flying —

Over the Cascade mountains, over Allan Brothers, and Black Sun,
we'll rise above the university and be back in time for tea, so get ready
                    to come flying —

Come out with me to Fall Creek, to the place where the islands part,
where we scaled rock and scree to find who we might have been
                    flying —

Come with your intense, your insistent gaze, come with silver
hair, and your body lithe and inspiring. The time is right, the landing
                    clear, come now!

Leave bright caution and computers and your excuses
in the wind. Today, before we're gone—
                    do come flying —

by Susan Rich
Inspired by "Invitation to Miss Marianne Moore" by Elizabeth Bishop

Chapter 15: It's A Piece Of Cake

I've traveled extensively and I've "traveled on my stomach." By that I mean that much of what I most remember from my trips has to do with food. White bread and butter won't give you much in the way of memory—unless it was the just-out-of-the-oven bread slathered with real butter and sugar that my great grandmother gave me.

Spend a few moments thinking about your childhood experiences with food as well as different meals you have had on vacations, day trips, or longer travels.

Here are several memories on my travels:

I ate plums on the street in Athens, the plums so ripe from a vendor on a sunny afternoon that the meat slipped out of their skins down my throat like red silver and down my fingers and arms like pink blood.

Barbecued caterpillars awaited us in Botswana after an afternoon of seeing giraffes and elephants, the dark settling, a fire blazing up, dinner soon in an outdoor tree house with ramps and stairs and a view from the trees. I ate half of my hairy morsel. My husband ate his own and my other half.

Then there's China and food. When I first taught at Shanghai Jiao Tong University in 2002, one of my students, Zhang Yagang, had written me a note to help me understand the importance of food in China: "From the north to the south in China, there are many kinds of special foods that are very different. For example, the foods of Jin taste sour, the foods of Chuan taste hot, and the foods of Yue taste sweet, etc. When you travel around China, there are some characteristic foods in the place where you arrive at. Besides good taste, these foods are very cheap. So I strongly recommend that you taste different foods of different region in China."

Here's a list poem from the menu at one of my favorite restaurants in Shanghia, just outside the gates of the university:

The Menu Tells Me Where I Am

Chilled jellyfish and turtle rim with Chinese broccoli
Duck's jaw in magi sauce
Steamed fish head with lam
Hundred-flowers sliced squid with spicy salt

Nourishing-lungs crocodile soup with sea coconut and tedrilleaf fritillary bulb
Arctic shell sashimi
Stewed teal with aweto
Salt leaching chicken feet
Delicious large fish head
Specialty stewed crocodile's foot in brown sauce
Australian scallop with nestle and seafood
Fresh assorted vegetables topped with winter melon soup
Be-for-time style eggplant
Celery with cashews and lily
Fried American calf ribs
and Tsingtao
Great Wall red wine

Think about specific memories you have with food and places. What are your top three favorite meals—what did they include? When you were young, did you have a certain special meal on your birthday or a favorite kind of cake? Does a certain food remind you of a parent or loved one? Did you ever order something in a foreign country only to be surprised by what they brought you?

Exercise 1: Baked Garlic Takes Me To Uncle Ed's House

Chip Hanlon from the Poynter Institute wrote a piece called "Writing with Your Nose." He lamented that no matter how much you hunted for scents, "You'll come up as empty as a bloodhound who's lost the scent."

Make a list of scents associated with food that you remember, such as:

> baking bread
> barbecued ribs
> beef stew
> buttered popcorn
> chili
> fried liver
> garlic
> melted chocolate
> fresh-cut rosemary
> chocolate chip cookies
> three-day-old fish

Write a poem that combines the scent with an experience:

Barbecued ribs at your Uncle Ed's house where Aunt Millie got drunk and misplaced her dentures and . . .

Making popcorn for your Friday night movies, your dad sets off the fire alarm and. . .

The liver your mother fixed once a month smelled up the kitchen, your stomach rising in your throat until. . .

(Poems can be inspired by a memory, but as a poet, you have "poetic license" to expand and exaggerate the story as needed.)

Exercise 2: When I Ate Steamed Clams

Ask yourself the following questions: What is your favorite food? Where and when do you usually eat it? Who fixed it or fixes it for you and when? What do you feel whenever you eat this food? Who have you eaten it with?

Food often is a symbol. Some of us eat macaroni and cheese when we need comfort food. We want a slice of white bread spread with raspberry jam like our mother made before she divorced. Some of us crave tortillas because our grandmother made them every Sunday. I eat oysters because I used to hate them and then came to love them pan fried, a reminder that things change.

For a jumping off point, begin your poem with the line:

"When I ate _____ the last time. . ."

Your poem can be an ode (a poem in praise of something), such as "Ode to Chocolate Cake" or "Ode to Gummy Bears." Use images, similes, and metaphors to describe how much you love this food. Include specific experiences or cultural references to the food you have chosen.

Exercise 3: At Sallie Mae's Café

Write a poem that focuses on the food you ate or prepared during a stressful or celebratory event. Maybe you remember a lunch date with your dad when the subject of your boyfriend came up, the advice he gave you that you've never forgotten. Or maybe you remember your family serving apple pie at your uncle's memorial because it was his favorite food.

To help you find images and ideas to use in your poems, make a list of at least ten things from that memory, such as time of day, what you did, sounds, colors, smells, and conversation:

—Drove with dad in the Buick
—Went to Sally Mae's Café
—Sat in a red booth by the window
—Ordered biscuits and gravy
—Dad said, "Now let's talk about that boyfriend…"

You can begin the poem with "I remember…" and go from there. You may want to remove the words "I remember" when you revise your poem.

Exercise 4: Peel And Chop

Make a list of words associated with food–utensils, process, etc. Here are a few to get you started:

boil, peel, candles, sauté, chop, scrape, forks, slow cooker, fry, spatula, grace before meal, steam, spoons, stir, knives, tablecloth, mince, timer, mix, whip, measure, pour, rinse, reheat, rice cooker, baking dish, layer, melt, toast, brown

Write a poem about a relationship that has nothing to do with food or about food, that doesn't have food in it, that doesn't even mention food, while using as many of the words from the above list as you can. You can also add your own cooking/meal words to the above list.

Poems To Inspire Your Work:

I FELL IN LOVE WITH A DOUBLE-YOLK EGG

In the egg
that cracked its head,
a tree and butterfly were dancing,
yellow wings, yellow leaves,
yellow, yellow—
breaking away from trunk. Who
painted all that yellow in there?
I'm falling in love with movement,
the swirl of yolk, a sapling hand

on the butterfly's back, a spin, a dip,
the swish of nucleus
flying into the rafters of bowl,
and here comes my lovemaking
hand, wanting to hold it all together:
how the egg and milk marry bread,
dressed in a dash of cinnamon.
Exotic, scented gown.
Polygamous ritual.
Eyes like ovenlight.
I disappeared into it all,
skipped across the rim of shell,
forgot my name and where I came from.
Hadn't I been to the source and back?
When they found me, I was dancing with apples
next to the handle of a floured pin.

by Melissa Studdard

☙

THE APPLE

Mother slices

the apple

without sawing

twirls out

the blossom end

the seeds with

one crisp swipe. Cross-

sectioned womb,

one for me, one

for sister.

Mother with one

hand open

and one fist clenched.

by Peggy Shumaker

☙

SUPER BABY JUMBO PRAWN

One up, one down, my favorite option
at the neighborhood taqueria,
and up and down again, a clunk

and a whisper: more perfect perhaps
if it were *shrimp*—pure ring
of oxymoron—but I like it

the way it is, with black beans
and green salsa, giant-minus-one
tortilla fresh from the steam. I like

the almost, the sideways, series built
and then broken: eleven or seven,
the abandoned factory with its grid

of mottled glass, in one corner
the inevitable birdsnest or bullethole.
Or the temptations of hopscotch—

step on a crack, break your mother's back.
I know, I know. How... expected,
how don't-we-always-want-it-

rough. Some days it's enough,
sitting in the car eating lunch,
watching surfers tempt the waves.

Sun through the windshield,
ice melting in the agua fresca.
And afterwards rolling bits of tinfoil

into tiny silver hearts, lightweight charms
strung out along the dash. Balance
of beans and rice, sting of salsa

where I bit my lip. Helpless,
compelled. I chew it till it bleeds.

by Lisa Gluskin Stonestreet

Chapter 16: You Can Quote Me

The following quotations give food for thought that require a bit of "chewing on." Bring your mind, body, memory, and feelings to these various quotations by famous individuals. They are windows into larger ideas about life, perhaps something that can't be as simple as some of the quotations imply.

Exercise 1: Disagreeing With Plato

Write a poem in response to one of the following quotations. Your poem can be a direct response, an argument, or a rant. For example, after reading Viorst's quote (number 1 below), I questioned whether a white lie is the same as a lie. A real lie. When I worked as a reporter, I was struck by the fact that if I asked five people at an accident scene what had happened, I heard five different stories. Not totally different but not the same. Were they lying? Is truth "incontrovertible," as Sir Winston Churchill claimed (number 2)?

Here is a list of ten notable quotations to choose from:

1. Judith Viorst:

    "I like the remark of a friend of mine who said, 'I'm willing to lie. But just as a last resort–the truth's always better."

2. Sir Winston Churchill:

    "Truth is incontrovertible, malice may attack it and ignorance may deride it, but, in the end, there it is."

3. Victor Hugo:

    "Where the telescope ends, the microscope begins. Which of the two has the grander view?"

4. Lao Tzu:

    "The Way of Heaven is to benefit others and not to injure. The Way of the Sage is to act but not to compete."

5. Plato:

> "I do not know how I may seem to others, but to myself I am only a small child wandering upon the vast shores of knowledge, every now and then finding a small bright pebble to be contented with."

6. E. B. White:

> "I wake up every morning determined both to change the world and have one hell of a good time. Sometimes this makes planning the day a little difficult."

7. Albert Einstein:

> "Gravitation is not responsible for people falling in love."

8. Chogyam Trungpa:

> "Live your life as an experiment."

9. Mahatma Gandhi:

> "An eye for an eye only ends up making the whole world blind."

10. Emily Dickinson:

> "I hope you love birds too. It is economical. It saves going to heaven."

I can't resist responding to several of the above quotations. For instance, I question Chogyam Trungpa about living "your life as an experiment. How can you "live your life as an experiment" when you don't have reliable data, a lab, or access to health care?

Here are starts of poems responding to two of the above quotations:

What about the telescope and microscope?
I'm willing to be inadequate
like a telescope that still can't center
on the farthest stars. But we are forced
into beliefs the first time we smelled blood,
forceps and human hands...

Dear Sir Winston,
I can see whales, jellyfish.
But truth, I've seen, can hide
under bushel baskets and cups.
After a practiced politician's hand
moves the baskets or cups, what,
pray, sir, is malice? Or truth?...

Now, choose a quotation from the ten examples and write your response as a poem.

Exercise 2: Cutting Circles (Instead Of Corners) To Save Money

Make up your own "famous quotation" that sheds truth or insight on life. Draw from personal experience and let the world know what you think about a given topic or situation. Maybe your quotation will be humorous or sad or hopeful or pessimistic. Your quote might be something like "If you can't find it in Wikipedia, it's not true…" or "It is better to have loved and not lost…" or "Early to bed, early to rise, makes me boring, quiet, and…".

Use your own "famous quotation" as the opening of your poem. Let your poem unfold as a response that either agrees with and further explains your quotation or you can play the devil's advocate and disagree with your quotation. Don't edit yourself—let your response or argument flow unimpeded.

Poems To Inspire Your Work:

SADNESS IS NOT A RIVER

Sadness is not a river that flows through the daily plain;
It is a flood that has overflowed its banks and reaches
Around every rock and deep into the roots of ferns
And Douglas fir, into crevices left by army ants and bees,
Where it sits soaking into the horizon waiting for a flame
To ignite the quiet depression that is drowning its victim
In the oil and kerosene of private immolation. Where is Joy,
The beautiful long-legged demon of youth that draws
The eyes of men and women alike? Where is June,
The queenly creature that soars through clouds, her fiery eyes

Ablaze with the spirit of sunrise? Gone, for Time has
Overflowed its aging banks, overwhelmed by the rush
That accumulates from months of snows. When day reopens
Its morning window, my mother rises like the winter sun,
Struggling through the foggy thoughts and ailing vision
That blur light and darkness into ordinary gray.
Although summer light has faded, the pain
Of rising and falling must sustain each day.

by Lonny Kaneko

8○

A WALK ALONG THE SNOHOMISH

I watch geese flock to the river's edge, stretch
their wings like the small ripples that slip
away with the tide. They duck their heads under,
lift one leg high. Stepping into a breath-
like fog, they could lean forward into the flat
line of the sky, touch the low sun warm

on the horizon. But today, my hands know only the warmth
of my pockets, the hole where the fabric stretched
thin, the cold touch which slows and thickens. The flat
slap of a wave becomes a loud echo. I feel sand slip
through the waves, a sigh pulled under,
pushed out. When I sleep, how do I remember to breathe

and exhale? How will my lungs catch the breath
escaping through my nose and my mouth? Warmed
by the small wisps of blue that grow on the under-
side of the sky, I want to look up into a stretch
of wings, count the feathers as they fall and slip
through the air onto my palm, across the flat

of my hand. Dappled light shimmers between the flat
boards of the bridge. The cold air whitens my breath
and a name I thought was forgotten slips
off my tongue, rising, then fading as it loses its warmth
to a sky too big to hold between outstretched
arms that have fallen to my sides. Under-

water reeds bend, pushed in one direction, and I think I understand why the Snohomish lies so flat,
why it seeks the lowest stretches
of land. Together, the geese lift up in one breath
but I don't know if they follow the sun because it warms
them or what they must feel as the earth slips

out slow and small. What I want to remember slips
from my mind. I can't see under
the water, past a reflection of warm
lights scattered in a woman's dark hair, lying flat
on the long smooth river. She doesn't breathe
or move her arms through this dull stretch

of ripples but drifts and slips silently under.
I feel the flat lungs in my chest stretch
out warm and expand. How quiet is the sound of my breathing.

by Sharon Hashimoto

☙

SUPERNOVA

A future sun will rise up in all its glory
so red and ravenous it devours the daytime sky,

matter ripping itself into sound and light
in one last explosion uncontainable as art itself.

Dying is an art, said Sylvia Plath,
dark energy providing the opposite of gravity.

Heaven performs a billion spectacular finales;
it's up to us to conjure the rest.

We'd all start with divinity and work backwards
if we could manage the math

but even Lady Lazarus burned her miraculous hair
in the calculus of resurrection.

Here at the table, event horizon flickering pink,
we begin with a sense of the absolute:

the emperor of ice-cream, Mrs. Ramsay's charm,
and light, of course,

the way it always travels at light speed.
Everything else is contingency—

cutlery glinting like a phantom,
peaches in a milk white bowl, figs going bloody blue.

by Mary Peelen

Chapter 17: When Grief Inspires

Marcel Proust wrote, "Happiness is beneficial to the body, but it is grief that develops the powers of the mind."

Really? Many times when we're in the middle of sadness—whether it's from grieving, being hurt, or feeling lost—we just want to get out of that misery. It's like being choked inside a shroud. And though we want to believe it when someone says, "It will get better," we're still in pain. Shakespeare wrote in Richard II, "Grief makes one hour ten."

Writing through grief is one way to explore feelings, taking what is hurting you and creating art. It can be healing to immerse oneself in poetry during grief. If you are grieving, the temporary world becomes "the new normal that isn't normal," says Kathy Munson, a counselor who believes it's good to grieve in whatever way you can. Sob. Feel morose. Feel sorry for yourself. Rant. Eat chicken soup. Eat chocolate. Listen to jazz. Sleep. Write.

And if you are not grieving, think back to a time you did grieve, and use those feelings to inform your poems.

Exercise 1: A Poem Of Loss

Write a poem about a time when you experienced a deep loss. This loss might have been a parent, a spouse, a relative, a pet, or perhaps a specific tragedy such as a flooded home or fire. Spend a few moments and return to that loss in your mind. Think back to the specific details of your story and take notes—go into your grief and put it out there on paper. Consider writing your poem in the first person ("I"), and let yourself go deep into the experience.

Exercise 2: Loss In Third Person

Write a poem about a deep loss in third person (she/he/they). In this poem, you are the observer witnessing the loss happening to yourself. Many times writing from the third person can give us the space to examine something that happened to us with less emotional attachment. For example, if you are writing a poem about your mother dying, don't begin with "When my mother died. . ." start the poem with "When her mother died. . ." As you write from this observer perspective, be sure to include specific images, avoiding abstract words such as grief, hurt, loss, sad, angry, etc. Show what you experienced in your poem through description, dialogue, actions, similes, and metaphors.

Exercise 3: My Sorrow Is Proud

Write a poem in which you give your grief a new identity. Think about a physical or emotional characteristic that isn't typically associated with sorrow, and write a poem where grief embodies that. For instance, we typically don't think of grief as being proud. But Lady Constance, in Act III of Shakespeare's *King John*, says this when she learns that her French and Austrian allies have deserted her to join forces with John:

> "I will instruct my sorrows to be proud;
> For grief is proud and makes his owner stoop.
> To me and to the state of my great grief,
> Let kings assemble; for my grief's so great
> That no supporter but the huge firm earth
> Can hold it up: here I and sorrows sit;
> Here is my throne, bid kings come bow to it."

Maybe your grief is wearing a court jester outfit and dancing on the railroad tracks. Maybe your grief is telling a joke and laughing. Maybe you want to sit down and have a conversation with grief—allow grief to take a human form and make its way in the world. This may be a good poem in which to incorporate magical realism—"when I came home from work, grief was sitting in the kitchen naked with a red hat and feathered boa, and she asked me for a glass of cabernet…

Exercise 4: Wild And Precious Life

Think about the opposite of grief. The last two lines of Mary Oliver's poem "The Summer Day" ends with:

> Tell me, what is it you plan to do
> with your one wild and precious life?

Write a poem that answers this question. Sometimes to deal with grief, we need to think "what if…" Consider writing your poem as a manifesto—a statement that sets out your goals or demands, your expectations, deadlines, strategies, and/or your philosophical stand. Use specific examples and powerful statements to show your reader what you want to *do with your one wild and precious life*.

Exercise 5: Grief In Three Lines

Because grief can feel large, try to contain that largeness in a small form by writing a haiku. You can use the standard haiku form which consists of a 3-line poem where the first line has 5 syllables, the second line has 7 syllables, and the third line has 5 syllables. You may want to simply write a 3-line poem choosing your own syllable count.

Here is a poem by Kobayashi Issa written about the death of his child:

This dewdrop world
Is just a dewdrop world
And yet

Your haiku can be about a specific person or a visual representation of what grief is to you. Also, if you find that one haiku is not enough space to explore your grief, consider writing a poem created from a series of linked haiku (or 3-line stanzas) as Catalina Cantu did in the poem below.

Poems To Inspire Your Work:

REFLECTIONS ON HOME / REFLEXIONES EN CASA

Climbing rose petals,/ Escalada pétalos de rosa,
pink as my cats ear, / rosa, como mis gatos oídos,
whisper welcome home. / susurro bienvenido/a casa.

Mom and I/ Mamá y yo
planted those roses,/ plantamos esas rosas,
40 years ago./ hace 40 años.

I was impatient to ride my bike, / Yo estaba impaciente por montar mi bicicleta,
to echo birds songs, / echo las aves canciones,
as trees spoke to me. / como los árboles me habló.

Today, I bury Mom, / Hoy, me enterrar Mamá,
with pine and roses. / con pinos y rosas.
I love you Mom./ Te amo Mamá

by Catalina Cantu

POMEGRANATE, RADIO ON
for Madeline DeFrees, 1919-2015

Begin with the fruit in your hands—
hold the weight of its rough skin,
its nested, cell interior.

Take your time.

Choose a lilac
blue bowl; pull your sharpest knife
from the cutlery drawer.

This has become your life, not the headlines

but the fine print
of the back pages. Read
slowly the small, good stories—

each seed another worldly

exchange. You're here
at the sink caressing—
there's no other word—

until the dazzling light lets go.

Until surreal tomorrows extend—
beyond sustenance, beyond juice,
stained fingers, stained news.

by Susan Rich

THE EARTH IS LOUD

Today is your 60th birthday and I
have lit a single candle, white and burnt from
the memorial service months ago. The sigh
of the earth is loud tonight and our baby comes
downstairs and says, "Mommy, I can't sleep,
the wind is too scary." My gone love, this is your
turf—consolation, kisses, "the pray my soul to keep,"
but you would not have said that—eschewing easy assur-
ance always, never atheist, but agnostic. I saw your
eyes as you died and cannot forgive myself. What
else I could have done? No matter. You aren't anymore,
and still, it is your birthday. Our book forever shut
on yesterday's page—this blue and windy end betrayed
our ever after—and yet, my love, Happy Birthday.

by Carmen R. Gillespie

℘

LIGHT GONE

Sleep holds
a child's hand

as memories
slide

into a black lake.

by Karen Lorene

Chapter 18: Invent-A-Word

I love dictionaries. I can get lost in them: Look up one word and a half hour later I've ended up going through many words. One of my favorites is *The Oxford Universal Dictionary*, a hefty tome of 2,515 pages. It first was published in 1933. The one I own, which belonged to my stepfather, was printed in 1955.

I also own a dog-eared paperback, *The Merriam-Webster* published in 1974, that I carried back and forth to my college classes for 27 years. I can't bring myself to give it away, or horrors, put it in the trash. Killing a dictionary seems like a sacrilege! Of the dozen or so other dictionaries I own, I refer most often to *Webster's New Collegiate Dictionary* of 1977, *Webster's Ninth New Collegiate Dictionary* of 1985, and the *Merriam-Webster's Collegiate Dictionary 11th Ed.*, 2003. The choice for me depends on where I'm sitting, as I have one at my elbow in my writing room, at the computer, at the table where I write each morning, in my travel bag, and in the glove compartment of my car. In addition to my paper dictionaries, I also look up words using online dictionaries.

Language changes. New words come into our dictionaries; some old words become archaic and can be found only in old dictionaries. "Paper," for instance, has been around a long time, but "zoodles," "kombucha," and "cryptocurrency" have only recently been added.

Consider the fact that the word "email" didn't appear in the *Oxford Universal Dictionary* in 1944. "Cursor" didn't exist then either; the closest word to it is cursory, an adjective that means "hastily and often superficially done."

In the 1974 *Merriam-Webster Dictionary*, the definition of mouse was "any of various small rodents with pointed snout, long body, and slender tail." In the *Merriam-Webster's Collegiate Dictionary, 11th Ed.*, the first definition of mouse remains basically the same, while its fourth definition is "a small mobile manual device that controls movement of the cursor and selection of functions on a computer display."

Here are a few words from the *Oxford Universal Dictionary* we don't see much, if at all, any more:

> "Hooping-cough" means a contagious disease chiefly affecting children; it's now spelled "whooping cough."

> "On live" is an earlier form of "alive."

"Yarely" means to walk promptly, briskly; it's now considered archaic.

"Yaw-yaw" means to talk affectedly.

"Xoanon" means a primitive rudely-carved image (originally wooden), especially of a deity.

Exercise 1: He's Acting Skilamalink

Spend time with a dictionary and find your own interesting word(s) or choose from the words listed below. Write a poem that explains the definition of your word(s) in a creative way. For instance, the archaic word "skilamalink" means secret or shady, so perhaps a poem using this word would describe a clandestine spy ring or a cheating lover.

> guzzault
> hawkstone
> hoodmatch
> preposenelle
> scroucher
> withonon

Exercise 2: It's Fabonderful

A "portmanteau" is a word that blends the sounds of two words and combines their meanings. The word "motel" is a portmanteau because it is a combination of "motor" and "hotel." Another example of a portmanteau is the word "brunch," which combines the words "breakfast" and "lunch."

To begin, write down at least twenty words that you either like or find interesting. Spend some time mixing these words into new words. "Fabulous" and "wonderful" can become "fabonderful," and "quiet" and "wisdom" can be combined to form "quisdom." Come up with at least six or seven portmanteaus and use all of these words in a single poem. Consider using one of them in your title.

Here is my poem using a portmanteau:

START WITH A PORTMANTEAU

Morpheme as smog from smoke and fog
mixing, matching the fabonderful
from a plethora of loanwords, borrowings, captions
derived from imagination and luck, repurposed
words that blast, tuggleshoot, turn
to opportunity. Tune fork the TV, pin up the window.
Seriously, have fun. Spread the word (pun
intended). Graft new words to your memory stick.
Send them to Oxford. Listen to them navigate the world.

Poems To Inspire Your Work:

DISPATCH FROM THE OFFICE OF THE CREATOR OF WORDS

They come in every day -- by mail, electronic and paper --
definitions in search of words, and it's my job to help.

They call me the logomancer, neologician, wordinator,
but I prefer holophrasist, for its sheer agoogleity. Ha!

Holophrasis: an entire idea expressed in a single word.
Adding that T was the easiest workday I've put in yet.

People want a word for the delight that crescendos
when hearing again a song you've just begun to love,

for that false silence in movie scenes filmed on jets,
for the opposite of shadow, for the baby living less

than a day, for clockwork: lights turning green right
before you brake, immediate boarding of infrequent train.

These are harder: The ways in which novels of ugly
men differ from those of handsome ones. The after-images

of a day of skiing, appearing just before sleep.
Of or related to words learned only after forty.

Enslavement of blondes by blondes. The look a woman
gives a man 20 years younger before she realizes she's

20 years older. The least amount of time to wait to wipe
a cheek after a too-enthusiastic kiss. The muddy way

our decade looks to pundits because it's now.
As I get to work, I'm paralyzed by the thought

of the malogist, he who calls each new word terrible.
But where would he be without my tribe? Wallowing

in mudgrunt, thinking few thoughts. Radarless,
unplugged, scubaless, unwired. Silent and alone.

by Tina Kelley

☞

PLEAPPY

I long for you to remove
that stiff upper lip,
frown of conundrum when
you're sitting between
two five-point harness car seats
and darned if you can find
the insertion location
for your own seat belt,
ice cream isn't the flavor
you ordered, a colony
of ants is taking over
your spice drawer,
your toddler keeps refusing
the antibiotics for strep,
you just got lambasted
on Instagram
and the PC police
take issue with you letting

your older children play with squirt guns,
such violence,
the pain in your wrist flares up,
and your first world fit
seems to call for UN funding
because of the whine
in your voice. This is a plea,
it is a please. Anyhow. Anyway.
I have a request. Pleappy.
I will assist in lifting your spirits.
Double team sunshine.
What would it cost you?
A personal serotonin boost!
Go for it!

by Mary Ellen Talley
Note: "Pleappy" is an invented word from the combination of "please be happy."

☯

APHASIA TESTING

Do two pounds of flour
weigh more than one?
Does the bugler have any friends?
If I'm not dead am I quick?

If words swim will I drown?
Will I drown friends if I pound?
Will one dead weight more tomorrow?
Will quick words bugle the brown fox?

If a hand can't cup, can it ballast?
Can a ballast weigh a prayer?
If I pray without words am I ceasing?
If I yes without nod am I no?

Are the lights on in this room?
Is one pound of flour heavier than two?
If I left my eye in my mouth is it right?
If I know what is nod will it show?

Is a hammer good for cutting wood?
If I could cord my vocal, would I?
Do I put on my socks before my shoes?
If I shush when I shatter will I shine?

by Michele Bombardier

Chapter 19: Fact Or Fiction?

Marvin Bell once said, "The I in the poem is not you but someone who knows a lot about you." While poetry is filed under "Nonfiction" in the library, not all poems are autobiographical; in fact when we read a poem we should consider the "I" in the poem as the "speaker" not the poet.

As poets we can bring true experiences to our poetry as well as creative fictional events. Your poem can mention that you had French toast for breakfast when in reality you had poached eggs or you can state in your poem that you skipped breakfast. Poems allow the poet to explore narratives by mixing fact and fiction.

Exercise 1: Two Truths And A Lie

Write a poem beginning with one of the sentences below—

>This is what I know about George Clooney...
>Welcome to the City called Morose...
>I love too easy. How do you learn to love hard?
>In my other life I was a tattoo artist...
>These days the moons hang like deflated balloons...
>On gray days I pray for sermons and sex...
>I was outside looking in...
>I stayed inside and looked out...
>I want to look up into a stretch of wings...
>The raccoons have built an inner city...
>I was not the last...
>I was the last...
>The volcano is past her scheduled eruption...
>Here is my hand...
>Daydreams have a lot of...
>The inner spaces are windowless...
>I had nothing but my dictionary...
>At a different time, in a different place...

Once you have chosen the line you want to start with, write a poem that incorporates various elements of your day that actually happened along with complete falsehoods that are in no way true.

For example, if you are writing about watching the moon rise from your bedroom window, you can include some facts about the moon, such as the exact length of its orbit around the earth. Next, you can include some false information—reaching up to take a slice of cheese from one of its craters as you sit in a tree house.

Allow this poem to move in and out of fact and fiction, as Cheryl Clayton's poem "Eleven" does, or consider writing a poem that is completely fictitious or derived only from factual information (like Tom C. Hunley's poem on page 94).

Exercise 2: The Poet Is Arrested

Write a poem in which every line is a lie, but attempt to make the poem sound believable, as if this poem is a slice of the speaker's true life. If you are writing in the first person in your own voice, compose lines that are false, but could seem true to your reader:

I was eating pie a la mode for breakfast
before the police broke open my front door
to arrest me for shoplifting granny smith apples,
cinnamon, and flour...

Exercise 3: The Earth Revolves Around The Moon

Write a poem in which you take a well-known fact (the earth is round, the sky is blue, $E=mc^2$, George Washington was the first president of the United States, birds have wings, etc.) and turn this fact into something that is false. For instance, write a poem that mentions Thomas Jefferson as being the first president of the United States or perhaps claim that Einstein discovered E=LOL. Your entire poem can be about this created falsehood, or you can simply slip in one false line ("When Einstein discovered E=LOL...") that will surprise your reader.

Poems To Inspire Your Work:

ELEVEN

Side by side, tall twin soldiers of the math battalion, second
in line of double digits following a round fat zero, companion

to a one. Eleven–slim, erect, with good posture stands still
before puberty when teens start the march toward a new decade.
Eleven is curious, begins to wonder how to get bigger and older fast,
how to get past twelve, launch herself into the exploration
of finding who she is and wants to become, trying many hats.
She doesn't know she could become a Roman numeral
with just an addition of one that looks the same as her twin.

by Cheryl Clayton

◊

MUSIVES AND A SILENT CRUMP

Musive was a fine word, the name of a moth, gone extinct.
Crump: the sound of a heavy shell or bomb. *Hurkle*: a crouching,
cowering motion. *Erump*: to erupt, burst forth. Were these words
phased out, slow, or did they surface and then disappear,
shy as whale backs? Maybe they entered and exited the language
in a rush, like *groovy, rad*, and *word up*, slang terms teens use,
then don't use, like hangouts turned "wack"
by the sudden arrival of parents. So many words,
but none for the smiles that flickered from Jane to me,

and back, when we'd reached a place in our life together
where we almost didn't need words. No word for
the strange joy I felt, cutting our firstborn son's umbilical cord
as he lay screaming on Jane's stomach. So many words,
but none tickled our infant son's throat.
Jane and I came to understand, this cry meant *I'm hungry*,
that one meant *burp me*, another meant *change me*.
Italians have seven words for "the," so why can't we
have words that distinguish a baby's different types of tears,

or a special words for the tears on Jane's face as she dug
her fingernails into her cheeks after he died in his crib?
Have you ever scratched someone, by accident,
as your arms grazed? I know the word for that. It's *scrazing*,
but I had no words to comfort Jane. *I'm sorry. It'll be okay.*
I knew these words didn't mean as much as I needed them to.

I had no words for the beasts eating my insides, musives
in a trunk full of clothes, no words for the hole I felt
and tried to fill with my writing, with my music,

with Camels and Jim Beam. And when Jane sought comfort
in another man's arms, when I found a red strand
of that man's hair on my pillow, on my bed,
when I was forced to imagine their wordless moans,
a silent crump shocked my senses, left me hurkling, unable to erump.
The words *cuckold* and *how could you?* and *I'll kill him*!
weren't there for me. *Wife* and *son* had turned into archaisms.
I had nothing but my dictionary, which grunted, signed, and shrugged,
a friend who had no words that could comfort me.

by Tom C. Hunley

Chapter 20: You Can't Write About Love

I tell my students: *You can't write about love and you can't end rhyme.* End rhyme waits for masters to use it well. As for love, there are too many pie-in-the-sky love poems without dirty socks, annoying habits, and farts.

But, when you're in the hands of masters, something magical happens—their "love poems" avoid the routinely romantic, the sappy melodrama, and the idealization of one's beloved. Good love poems look at the concept of love through real-life examples, unique images, humor, disappointment, gratitude, and sometimes even anger.

Exercise 1: My Non-Detailed Beloved

Write a love poem that takes place in a specific location—a boat, New York City, a physics class, a kitchen, a bus terminal, a rain-soaked field, a specific street like First Avenue, a graveyard, or a Burger King (note how the poem will change if you use the restaurant in the Ritz-Carlton instead of Burger King). Describe the place but don't describe your beloved. Work on tone: contemplative, loud, didactic, humorous.

For example, think of a train station:

I hear the two beams of light
shining down their tracks, baby,
my face a ghost in the steam,
you and me...

Exercise 2: I Love You Because You Don't...

Write a love poem that is also a list poem. Address your poem to a specific person and list the ways you love him/her/them because of what he/she/they *doesn't* do. Here are a few example lines:

Because you don't hate my mother's eight long-haired cats
Because our kitchen sink has days of dishes
Because my tarot cards don't spook you

Aim for at least twelve to fifteen "because" lines. At the conclusion of your poem, break the "because" pattern and end with an example of why you love him/her phrased in the affirmative without the use of "because":

You are the thunder that shakes the ocean awake.

Poems To Inspire Your Work:

IS LOVE A MOMENT LOST IN VERTIGO

Is love a moment lost in vertigo?
The dizzy spells appear and disappear.
Let's dare the old physician to say it's so.

The day I learned to kiss you on the nose,
the world tipped and spun me on my ear.
Is love's best moment lost in vertigo?

As long as I could stand and dream, I'd know
my feet were firm, and then you smiled and shared
the words the old physician gave to you: so

long as passion fuels the body, throws
the heart off stride, and chews the cords of nerves,
love may be overcome by vertigo.

Almost forty years we've bloomed like roses
caught in a hurricane. Age repairs.
Let's dare the old physician to tell us so.

This world's a crazy top, a dizzy show;
our love will grow a hundred years, and more.
Love's no moment lost in vertigo.
I bid the old physician to say it's so.

by Lonny Kaneko

☙

LOVE NOTES
Huachuca Mountains, Arizona

i W.H. Frierson—1855-
1928—lies here, his mining pick's
iron head centered
at the foot of his tombstone, creekside,
just off the trail. Those dates,
he could have heard Geronimo in the snap

of a twig. Lovers of rust, we wander
his cabin's remains: scattered planks
pointing toward a porch, a banjo song.
We water up, having almost
played out this vein.

ii Potent in blue air
just across the saddle between canyons,
nine-foot stalk of agave
rises. Thick as a thigh, it strains
to burst into flower. Beside its base
of spiked flaring leaves we sway,
sweat-soaked, shadowless.

iii They dart and swoop
high above the crag where we sit
with Jarlsberg and apples, white-throated swifts,
six or seven of them, tails forked. One
dives toward another and they fuse. The tiny

mass plummets into the canyon. Half a breath
from the creek bed below us
they fly apart.

by John Willson

Chapter 21: Leaping Poetry

The term *jumping Jehoshaphat* was used to express astonishment. It is first recorded in Mayne Reid's book titled *Headless Horseman* in 1866, but many claim it has biblical roots. Leaping poetry is an imaginative leap into an imaginary place, which takes a reader from an image or word to a place we could not foresee. We are taken from "an image" that is, according to Robert Bly, "simply a body where psychic energy is free to move around."

In Bly's book *Leaping Poetry: An Idea with Poems and Translations*, he maintains that we have three brains: the reptile, which is all about survival; the mammal, which fills up most of our skulls and is about sexual love, ferocity (and includes rock music); and the new brain with its wild spiritual ideas. The mark of the new brain is light, and he uses Bach (composer) and Blake (poet) as examples. Bly argues that people should try living in each brain and that "a poet could try to bring all three brains inside poems."

Leaping poetry in the hands of poets such as Federico Garcia Lorca, Antonio Machado, Naomi Shihab Nye, Anna Akhmatova, Robert Bly, Anne Sexton, James Wright, W. S. Merwin, and Ellen Bass, among many, transports and astonishes us. Words such as *dragon smoke, terror, whirling, sleeping snow, calyx, stung and headless horseman* in the poems of certain poets connect us to something inexplicable—from associations deep in our mammal brains to new and unexpected understanding in another realm.

Leaping poems often are anchored by their titles: "Winter Scene" by Marguerite Young, "Blood" by Naomi Shihab Nye, "Walking Around" by Pablo Neruda, "A Green Stream" by Wang Wei, and "Landscape with Two Graves and an Assyrian Hound" by Federico Garcia Lorca. These poems depend on specifics such as cold tulips, white ptarmigan, fig, table mat, elevators, Monday, rapids, nut-horns, feather, sheets. But as the poets use an image or images, they go deeper into the idea or movement lying beneath, and through metaphor they make a leap into something more powerful—like being shot out of earth's orbit into space. With this technique, the poems are both grounded and flying! Quite a magician's trick!

Leaping poetry is a way to surprise your reader (and hopefully yourself as well) by allowing the imaginative jumps in your poem to take your reader somewhere surprising and unexpected.

Exercise 1: From Paprika To Ghosts

Write a poem that moves from an ordinary event into the extraordinary. Think about something you do such as make chili, rake leaves, brew beer, do laundry, drive to the grocery store, write a letter to your mother, watch your daughter's soccer game, or talk with your father who has Parkinson's. Use specific details in your poem—for example, if you were writing about making chili your poem may include the types of beans you used, how long it simmered on the stove, and several spices you added. Allow one of these expected details to lead you to an unexpected place by using the word "as"— "as I add a tablespoon of paprika to the chili, I see the ghost of my dead father in the doorway. . ." Or maybe the unexpected is in the speaker's mind, so your line could read "as I add a tablespoon of paprika to the chili, I remember how my grandmother put spices in the graves of her pets..." As you continue to write, allow the small details in your poems to make large leaps into other topics or subjects.

Exercise 2: Flying Sofas

Tomas Tranströmer begins his poem "Late Autumn Labyrinth" with fields and rusty machines. He moves to "A letter from America," where "evil and good actually have faces" and people rule from glass where "Violence seemed unreal." The "walking trees" were caught in the glass. A plane comes in that casts a shadow "like a giant cross" over a man in the field. He's seen the cross in church vaults, he writes, like "a split-second shot of something." This poem travels within a large labyrinth that gives specifics and, again, that sense of "other worldliness."

Write a poem that starts with a concrete image of a landscape and moves into a letter. While Tranströmer starts in a field and writes to America, your poem could begin with a visual of a mountain range and a cloud in the shape of a rocket before it moves to a letter to your lover. As you write, create adjective/noun combinations that you don't normally see together such as Tranströmer's "walking trees." Your poem may include "quartz flagpoles" or "misunderstood bridges." If you want, make a list of at least ten of these adjective/noun word combinations before you begin your poem, and include as many as possible.

Poems To Inspire Your Work:

WHAT I KNOW

Hummingbird wings buzz silent,
soft blades trap my watchful gaze.
Flowers whistle open all around,
lifting their petaled skirts, exposing
their soft parts. Bad things
can happen any moment.
They happen every day.

                    We may start another war.
                    We may build walls

along every border,
but spring knows nothing of this. Spring,

                    that harlot,
                    will not shake off the wet
                    for the sun

or release summer's coattail
for a drop of rain. She is fickle,
a Gemini balanced between
wanting the best of both. Worlds
for a hummingbird is the distance

                    from flower   to flower,
                    tree   to tree.

This fruit tree stands straight and bare in my garden,
yet it entreats. The humming bird

                    hovers and dips,
                    rises and falls,
                    like the last breaths of the dying,

until both flower and bird are satiated.
Suffering occurs in a shutter speed,
death in a sneeze, but
spring will warm a grave
as easily as it warms this garden.

This is what I know of God—
the continuing on.

by Jamaica Baldwin

OLD MAN FOLDING A KERCHIEF IN THE SUPERMARKET
   for Hayden Carruth

He has used it to wipe the filth
from the table where his daughter
has left him to do her shopping
spilling it from the pocket of his jacket
like a small blue lake
the color of an old house dress.

Now he is folding it back into shape
with blunt fingers, hunched
over his labor, watching intently
his hands as though
they might betray him.

For ten minutes this has been
his whole work, & he has gathered
all the deliberate threads
of his attention into this single
act, oblivious to the fact
that anyone might be watching,
that he might be teaching us all
how to live.

by Samuel Green

THE MAGICIAN

Death, and the hint of it, waves its wand.
When I walk, everything shimmers—
the frayed needles of a cedar
outlined against unseasonable blue
of a northwest sky.
A dogwood lit as if a cloud of white butterflies
parachuted like handkerchiefs
to cover it. The red-winged blackbird's
trill, elixir of song—stunning.

Other times revelation hits like a swarm
of gnats, then, as if I were sawed in two.
It comes as gravity, calling me
to my knees, to prayer,
for my son: the dystrophy of his muscles
missing proteins, his falling over
air, slipping, away.

Death waves its wand at both of us.
Like a hummingbird's rush of wings,
beating, beating, it hovers
in front of my heart,
sticky nectar of grief. It circles
overhead waiting to perform
its cutting act.

by Suzanne Edison

Chapter 22: Outside And Inside Out

We're always looking around us, because we're curious and because we want to be safe. "Look both ways before you cross the road," your mother shouted as you went to board the school bus. "A saw has no friends," your grandfather said when you used a saw for the first time.

We look out of windows and doors. We look into screens–TV, cell phone, movie, computer–and into books, magazines, shop windows, our refrigerators. We look under hoods, seats, box lids. We open letters, cereal boxes, wallets, and backpacks. Sometimes we see what we expected. Sometimes we're surprised, and not always in a pleasant way. But we're always looking.

Exercise 1: Cats And Worries

Start outside and look out into your world through a window or door or into your TV, computer screen, or refrigerator. Describe what you find. Make a list of six observations and use plenty of detail:

—large leaf maple spreading its branches with leaves on one branch turning yellow
—neighbor's black and white cat Jasper chasing her tail
—moldy cheese, jar of mayo, and leftover pizza
—a protest march near the White House
—a long line of cars behind the afternoon school bus
—a new season of your favorite show on Netflix to binge-watch on the weekend

Now look inward into yourself. Describe what you are thinking, feeling, remembering. Make a list of six items. Again, be specific:

—a memory of being lost near the play equipment in the city park
—experiencing the taste of sushi for the first time
—a friendship that recently ended with an argument
—worry about finances and paying for the mortgage and car
—feeling tired because of being out late on a great first date
—wondering how to rearrange the furniture to create a warmer atmosphere

Choose an item from each list and tie together your "outside view" with an "inside" memory or experience in a poem. Choose the experiences that evoke the most energy and enthusiasm.

Exercise 2: Disagreements And Condiments

Using your two lists that you have created, quickly think of a number between 1 and 6. If your number is 3, for instance, write a poem that combines the third item on your "outside" list with the third item on your "inside" list. Using the above list examples, the poem for this exercise would combine "moldy cheese, jar of mayo, and leftover pizza" with "a friendship that recently ended with an argument."

Poems To Inspire Your Work:

ON THE TEN-YEAR ANNIVERSARY OF A FRIEND'S DEATH

I loved watching you at your son's bar mitzvah,
how thrilled you were that you made it,
a sign, you said, from God
that the world would hold him up.
When I look at the pictures of that day,
you are smiling and his mouth is a rounded *oh*,
he is getting your bold eyebrows
(back when you had eyebrows, you'd say).

Maybe I've already passed, you said that fall
as we sat on your patio drinking cider,
the autumn sun on our shoulders.
You said you felt the others
who had already crossed. You leaned
forward to better look into my eyes,
don't stop talking to me, after.

Have I been a good friend?
Our conversations now are so short.
But I feel you especially in September.
I still borrow your faith.
I light the beeswax candle

on the mantle, watch the leaves
fall from big leaf maple,
open the window, and listen.

by Michele Bombardier

☙

THERE ARE SO MANY THINGS

I've already forgotten
the farmer, her empty jars, bees

littering the ground. So many gold coins.
Some, I raked into fire, listened as they

sizzled. Some, I arranged in fans
as a headstone for my father, who remains nameless

until the money comes in. Whistling Pete,
Ground Bloom Flower, Black Cat – how many

ways must I return to this story of soot?
Each birthday another funeral, a means

of burying you deeper. Look into the distance:
I'm the one on the water, waving

flashcards to guide you. Over there,
the mountain rises above cargo ships, harbor

lights. And over here, my echo of sea.
Ferry, ferry, ferry. Wave over wave

over wave. There is no honey dark enough
to bring us a shine of coin, no marriage

sweet enough that death won't return
dragging its coral bag of expectations.

by Ronda Piszk Broatch

☙

HER FATHER WAS A PAIR OF BINOCULARS IN THIS METAPHOR

Through you she glances
back at sparkling Seattle sharpened
to sharpest clarity and framed
in the black circle of your paired barrels,
or gazes at the sun reflected twice, in glass
and flat water, her palms against
the sturdy black, yes, elegant plastic.
Because she can, she dangles
you around her neck, where you bang,
bang against her heart.

by Pamela Carter

Chapter 23: In Praise Of Everything

Anything can be inspiration for a poem—fruit, vegetables, a stone you find on the street, a leaf, a hammer, an empty can of soda, a bowl of pistachios. What makes these items even more inspiring for our poems is that we can physically hold or touch these items, and find new ways of looking at them.

Sometimes the items we write about connect themselves to a poet. For example, plums and red wheelbarrows remind us of William Carlos Williams, while wild geese bring to mind Mary Oliver. Concrete nouns are all around us, and we get to decide which ones we want to write about. Pablo Neruda wrote a collection of poems called *Odes to Common Things* in which he explores the items that surround him in his daily life. Some of the things he writes about are socks, soap, bread, cats, and tables—showing us how everyday items can be fodder for poems. (Odes are poems that are written in praise and celebration of something or someone.)

Some poets like to carry a notebook to make a list of specific items they encounter throughout the day. Linda Bierds referred to these items in her notebook as "orphaned images,"—images she has encountered that are looking for a home in a poem.

Exercise 1: Up Close With A Potato

Speaking of ordinary items, did you know that eight potato species with thousands of varieties grow in the Andes, the second highest mountain range after the Himalayas? Or that potatoes are a member of the nightshade family, and a number of those members, such as Belladonna, are highly poisonous?

Potatoes are also known as spuds and varieties include Adirondack Red, Blue Congo, Golden Wonder, Lady Balfour, Selma, and Yukon Gold. Potatoes have fiber, as well as Vitamin C, potassium, and other minerals. Vodka is made from potatoes, but also French fries and potato chips. Hasbro began selling Mr. Potato Head in 1952.

For this exercise, we're going to get close and personal with a potato. (Note: if you don't have a potato, choose another fruit or vegetable you have access to.) Hold your item and take a few moments to describe its physical features. What does it look like, smell like, feel like, etc.? Now, cut it open, if possible. What happens when you cut the potato/fruit/veg.? Take a small bite and chew it. Describe the taste. Once you have spent some time with your potato (or other item), write a poem called "Ode to a Potato (or Banana or Onion, etc.)" in which you speak about the specific details of the fruit/veg. Use as many of your senses as possible to describe the item.

This exercise can be altered slightly and used with any concrete nouns to write odes to everyday things (wine, cats, tuna, socks, artichokes, etc.) as Pablo Neruda did.

Exercise 2: My Shoe On The Great Wall Of China

Write a poem where you take a series of everyday items and put them in not-so-everyday scenarios. You could place a pair of bedroom slippers floating down the Mississippi River on a log or begin your poem with a tube of toothpaste on the red carpet of a famous movie premiere. Be imaginative as your poem unfolds with images of everyday items in unique and surprising locations.

Poems To Inspire Your Work:

POTATO EYES

We push without legs, like cocoons
the color of maggots inveigling
our way past pill bugs, worms,
antennae reaching for the feel
of rain, not just wetness but for
the music of it, by now our eyes
opened, unfurling. We lie
like a memory, waiting for the spade.
We keep our nightshade
family to ourselves, pockets growing
among the soil and millipedes, stones
singing their own stories of kingdoms
and uprisings, the potato eaters, miners
and stone masons, all of them knowing
by the sweat of their brows.

by Susan Landgraf

WE HOLY THIEVES

At night I write to you
Because the moon's fullness
Is a bad accident, and I
Need to travel halfway
Across Texas, driving
In reverse. Our love
Is a screech owl; we
agree on that
Much. I'm miles past
Livingston, past
Nacadoches. The darkness
Gasps with the blush
Of sunrise. Nobody
Recognizes what is
So obviously blooming.
The beautiful part   is you.

by Robin Reagler

Chapter 24: Questions Without Answers

You may remember, or not, how many questions you asked as a child. But if you have raised a child, you remember. If you are a teacher you have experienced question after question after question. On and on. All day long.

>   Why can't I have a candy bar?
>   Why do people get sick?
>   Where did I come from?
>   Why do birds have wings?
>   Why don't I have wings?
>   Where does the sun go to sleep?

Some of the above questions can be answered in a factual manner, but some can only be answered using a response that finds its source in creative imagination. For instance, a mother can explain to a child why a candy bar might not be the best food to consume, but some imagination must be invoked to answer "Where does the sun go to sleep?" A creative response might go something like this: "Each night the sun falls asleep in the arms of the constellation Orion, the hunter. He sings a lullaby, and then tucks the sun into bed."

Exercise 1: Do Trees Whisper To Each Other?

Write a list of questions that you might have asked as a small child. It's ok if you do not remember the questions in detail. Remembering yourself as a child, what sorts of questions might you have asked? Maybe when you were small you were fascinated with dolphins. Maybe you once asked "Do dolphins cry saltwater tears?" Once you have three or four questions, choose a question to be the theme of your poem. You can begin your poem with a phrase like, "As a child I always asked (insert your question here)," and then the rest of your poem can respond to the question. Perhaps your question is answerable with facts, or perhaps your question will take some imagination and creativity to answer.

Exercise 2: My Hair Is Shouting

Write a poem that attempts to answer one of the following questions. Your poem can also explore the question without giving a definitive response. For instance, you could explore the wonders of chocolate without specifically saying *why* it is addictive and delicious—fudge, mousse, tiramisu, truffles, mocha, cookies, etc.

> Why is chocolate so addictive and delicious?
> Have extraterrestrials ever visited our planet?
> What would your hair say to you if it could talk?
> What would the world be like without the color red?
> Is there proof that there is an afterlife?
> Do dreams ever foretell the future?

Exercise 3: What If Amy Winehouse Were Still Alive?

Write a poem that consists entirely of questions. Choose a word/phrase to repeat as your opening for each question. You can choose from one of the following (or come up with your own):

> What if…
> How…
> Is it true that…
> Who is…
> Where do…
> When will…
> Why do…
> Is my…

Aim for at least fifteen questions, and don't worry about giving any answers. Don't edit your questions too much, but let them flow from your subconscious. Once you have finished your poem, consider rearranging some of the lines for a smoother flow. What kind of answer is the poem itself giving by how it's ordered? Here are a few example lines:

> What if you had left me after the argument during the camping trip?
> What if I now lived by myself in an apartment in the city?
> What if my living room had only orange furniture and orange walls?
> What if I stayed up until 2 am each morning writing romance novels?
> etc.

Poems To Inspire Your Work:

POEM FOLDED INTO A BOAT AND OFFERED TO THE BOGUE FALAYA

Where will words take me today

and where, silent waters, will you ship the words

From what troubles shall I be lifted

What will you show me

What do birds speak of in the wet grass

On this journey, how many footsteps,

how many crickets shall I scatter

If I crouch like this how long

before a fox brushes past

How long since fog lifted its net

and released my soul to leap

by Alison Pelegrin

ೞ

BROKEN SONNET: DIVORCE

I never knew the birds
The way she did-
To me, a cormorant appeared
To be an egret who shed
All his colors for black.
I forget if herons

Will mate for live. Do the males flock,
Or do they fly alone?
I need to find the name
Of the one who leaves the land behind,
Making flight his home.
The wind will choose which feathers line a nest
And which glide into mist.

by Michael Spence

ಬ

A BRIEF AND SORDID HISTORY OF THE SPECULUM:
Dr. Sims Use Of Enslaved African Women As Experimental Subjects

Tell me Doctor Sims,
how many women did it take?
In truth
you need not remember.
You see memory
is the mosquito mummified
in tree sap.
Its fragile body shrewdly sheltered.
Intact.
Unmolested
by time and men and you,
sir. We remember you.
We carry your "progress" in our blood,
passed down through generations
of women. Our ancestor's
unrequited rage rattles our cells.
This is our cancer
sir. Confess.
What did you tell your children?
What memories did they bequeath
to their sons?
No,
you need not explain.
I've seen it in their eyes.
These men I stumble into sometimes,

going about my day—
know. Not in their minds,
but in the sap of their cells. They know
they've muscled their way
into the deepest seas,
parted them, played God
for a while then left it there.
Sometimes when I look in these eyes
I see yours that held me
captive on your table,
naked, legs pinned back
like a frog prepared for dissection
and when this happens I'm certain
these men carry your afflictions
inside them. If I pried them open doctor
believe me,
they'd remember who I am.

by Jamaica Baldwin

Chapter 25: The Shapes In Our Poems

We know our world, in large part, because of its shapes. A box can be a square or rectangle, but an orange is round. The moon can be round, but it also can be cradle-shaped. An "R" could hold water because it has closure, but an "S" could not.

One of a child's first "learning" toys is a "shape game," whether it be a Playskool version or measuring cups out of the kitchen cupboard. The lesson: A circle cannot go into a square hole. In mathematics, young learners find that even though the following signs both use two lines, an "x" is not a "+". Knowing each shape carries a different meaning makes all the difference in whether a wall stands up or falls down, if we're adding something together or putting an "X" in a box.

Exercise 1: An Oval Named Nancy

Draw a shape. Any shape, letter, symbol, etc. Consider the following or come up with one of your own:

square, R, circle, rectangle, knot, V, oval, treble clef, lightning bolt, S, ≠, ∞, ♀, $, ?, spiral, diamond, &, !, etc.

Write a personification poem about that shape. (Personification refers to attributing human characteristics to an inanimate object, or in this case, a shape.) Consider naming your shape: Spike, Ink Blotch, Samantha, George, etc. Describe your shape and give it a personality. Is your treble clef tall and likes to eat guacamole while sitting on the couch watching reality TV? Is your circle named Sassy, and it feels powerful because of its roundness and smoothness?

Exercise 2: Dear Icosahedron...

Geometric shapes sport some of the greatest names. Say the following aloud:

> equilateral triangle (3 equal sides)
> isosceles triangle (2 equal sides)
> trapezoid (2 lines parallel, 2 lines not)
> pentagon (5-sided)
> hexagon (6-sided)

nonagon (9-sided)
polygon (any 2-dimensional shape formed with straight lines.)

Write a poem to one of the names of the above shapes or one of your choosing. Begin the poem by writing, "Dear _____" (insert name of the shape you've chosen) and explore what is wonderful and/or perplexing about this shape. For example, if you choose the trapezoid, you might begin:

Dear Trapezoid,
Some say you're difficult
to understand, what with words
like parallelograms and rectangles
and the fact that you can have right angles…

Poems To Inspire Your Work:

L'ESCARGOT
after the gouache-on-cut-and-pasted paper by Henri Matisse

On his deathbed, Matisse
       arranged these gouache cutouts.
See, the blocks in their loose spiral
       touch: loden-tangerine-pumpkin-
tangerine-lemon-lilac-black-loden;
       so like one animal's ability
to go linear or coil back. Answer
       without, answer within.
His last work: a snail whose spiral-
       ling can never be tracked.

by Janée J. Baugher

ಌ

THE POINTED TREES

You came out of the door in the cliff, the red cliff where the People had lived. You said *had dwelled* like *well*, but there were none: their water came from the river. Red sand. *Pueblo.* I climbed in, thinking there would be a stove and a chair, but the air was as still as the way you look at someone and you both know something will happen.

Here is a house. Rectangles of panes, roof, grass—something one can breathe in. Nature is not rectangular but the eye loves it—glass right-angled and sharp as sky, purer than liquid iris, cowlicked hair, soft creased mouth.

Now the people in their wool coats have climbed into a wagon but there's no horse to pull them, just a backdrop of pines and sky that appears over the water—there are the dunes there is the ocean.

We float the blue dinghy in the shallows. The sand shimmies when the flounders move. I ask *is a flounder a sole* and you ask *soul like angel* and I say you always spell *angle*.

The girl returns with a rabbit slung from her belt, her face solemn, rifle in her mittened hand, boots caked with snow. *The rabbit is good, a good one*, the elders nod, *its pelt a new hat, its flesh food.* The rabbit is good, the girl is good, the pointed trees behind her so lovely the world can hardly stand it.

by Arlene Naganawa

Chapter 26: Seedlings and Starts

All four of my grandparents could grow anything. My mother's mother grew roses without blight, green beans that weighted their stems, and rhubarb with elephant ear sized leaves. Inside, she kept a Christmas cactus that always bloomed twice a year. Her African violets competed with each other to produce the most blooms in her bay window. It was a riot of plants. She was a master at growing them from cuttings and seedlings.

Consider tomato seeds. In order for them to grow, someone will have to:

—sow seeds in seed-starting mix
—watch for germination after the seventh day
—take newborns out of their communal beds and transplant each in its own container
—put the containers outdoors when the weather has warmed to acquaint them with the sun, starting with a few hours at a time
—plant each tomato plant in a hole in the garden
—pat the soil firmly around each plant's root.

Obviously tomato seedlings, or any seedlings, don't go out and make it on their own without work and some tender, loving care. Like poems.

Exercise 1: Starting With A Start

Begin with one of the following "seeds" or "starts" and see what kind of poem unfolds and grows. Try to limit your poem to ten lines and be sure to use vivid detail in your descriptions. Here is your list of "starts":

> The last time I saw you...
> I didn't mean to break the...
> Falling, falling...
> After the birds came...
> With a book and a pair of sunglasses...
> Remember the time we...
> I was surprised when you...
> The talking crow in the pine...
> When I got your text...
> Don't say those words...
> When the lights went out...
> They used to say...

Whenever the moon...
You remind me of...
I used to believe in luck...
When you cry about...

Exercise 2: A Mad Carnivorous Plant

In keeping with the theme of plants, seeds, and starters, write a poem that uses an actual plant as an image for an emotion or state of being. Your starting line can include the emotion and the plant, for instance, "My anger is like a Venus flytrap..." or "Love is an ornamental cabbage..." Allow your poem to explore the similarities between the emotion and the plant:

My anger is like a Venus
flytrap catching gnats on black
bananas, digesting them slow and...

The following two lists contain emotions/states of being and plants. Use items from the lists to compose your poem or come up with your own emotion and plant.

Emotions/States of Being:

love, jealousy, joy, anger, sadness, paranoia, peacefulness, fear, anxiety, excitement, gratitude, depression, boredom, etc.

Plants:

palm tree, rose bush, moss, poison ivy, daffodil, tulip, maple tree, redwood tree, seaweed, dandelion, crab grass, lettuce, sagebrush, buttercup, etc.

Exercise 3: Tracing It Back To The Seed

When we look back at the origin points of some of the decisions, outcomes, or events in our lives, we often say, "The seed of _____ was planted when _____." For instance, a writer might say, "The seed of me becoming a poet was planted when I was a child, and I compared the setting sun to a beach ball. I began thinking in images after that experience." Think about an aspect of your life where you can find the origin point, the seed, and write a poem inspired by the planting of that seed and the result of its growth and maturity. Your poem can focus on something positive in your life (like becoming a creative writer) or on something difficult (the seed that led to chronic anxiety, for instance).

Poems To Inspire Your Work:

A THING I KNEW

A bird is a spirit.
A flock: a scarf of singing.

A black wren
will take my troubles in,
rattling pea vines, needle eyed.

by Arlene Naganawa

☙

THE SECRET OF SOIL

The secret of smoke is that it will fill
any space with walls, no matter
how delicate: lung cell, soapy bubble
blown from a bright red ring.

The secret of soil is that it is alive—
a step in the forest means
you are carried on the back
of a thousand bugs. The secret

I give you is on page forty-two
of my old encyclopedia set.
I cut out all the pictures of minerals
and gemstones. I could not take

their beauty, could not swallow
that such stones lived deep inside
the earth. I wanted to tape them
to my hands and wrists, I held

them to my thin brown neck.
I wanted my mouth to fill
with light, a rush of rind
and pepper. I can still taste it

like a dare across a railroad track,
sure with feet-solid step. I'm not
allowed to be alone with scissors.
I will always find a way to dig.

by Aimee Nezhukumatathil

☞

EXPECTATIONS

Last time I saw Zubia,
air hung thick as ripe
grapes ready for wine, filling
the air with desire.

Nights were slow to darken,
white walls glowing
in the moonlight, grapes
splitting their skins, dropping

to dust. There were more
grapes than people to eat them.
More desire than people knew
how to fill, want flowing

down the walks, spilled
wine turned dark
rivers and the grasses,
drunk with abundance, chafed

the wind. That was my last
night in Zubia, mythical
kingdom of imagination, pearl
of the deserted page.

by Susan Landgraf

Chapter 27: Thinking in Similes

Albert Einstein said, "Life is like riding a bicycle. To keep your balance, you must keep moving," and Horace Mann said, "A house without books is like a room without windows."

We seem to be born simile makers! A simile compares one thing to another, using "like" or "as." Simile is derived from the Latin word that means "similar." We find similes everywhere in our day-to-day language.

Some examples of similes are:

> Happy as a clam.
> Life is like a box of chocolates.
> Driving like a bat out of hell.
> The tunnel was dark as coal.
> The moon is like a round of yellow cheese.

Similes make poems richer by creating surprising comparisons and by giving abstract concepts a concrete and relatable form. The challenge of using similes in poems is to avoid clichés by coming up with unique associations. We have all heard "Happy as a clam," but have we come across "Sad as a root-bound spider plant?"

Exercise 1: This Poem Is Like...

Below are some prompts to help you create similes. Complete the phrase to make your own unique association, and feel free to come up with more than one simile per prompt. For example, if the prompt reads "The waves sounded like:" you may write several comparisons, such as "a freeway" or "a whisper" or "someone dropping ten gallons of paint from my apartment window." And remember to avoid clichés!

> Running after a bus makes me breathe like...
> Branches reach up as...
> An "S" is like...
> I'm as tired as...
> The stars are shining like...
> Sometimes my life is like...
> This cheese smells as...
> The child practicing the trombone sounds like...

Falling asleep is like…
The number 9 looks like…
Oysters taste like…
Red is to blue as…
Regret is like…
My sadness is sometimes like…

Choose your favorite similes from your list above, and write a poem that incorporates as many of them as possible.

Exercise 2: Wind Like A Bugle

Write a poem in which you imitate Emily Dickinson's poem "There Came a Wind like a Bugle" (see poem below), using modern day images and comparisons. For example, maybe your poem begins, "There came a Wikipedia entry like a Buzzfeed…" or "There came an Uber car like a lightning bolt…" Your poem can parody Emily Dickinson or you can directly imitate her poem beginning with the opening line.

Another possibility for your poem is to choose images from "There Came a Wind like a Bugle" and write your own similes, such as "the grass quivered like a. . ." or "the green chill passed like a . . ." or "the emerald ghost looked as…" or "the panting trees are like…" or "the steeple bell sounded as…"
Use Dickinson's poem as inspiration by creating new and unique similes from her images and working them into your poem.

THERE CAME A WIND LIKE A BUGLE

There came a Wind like a Bugle–
It quivered through the Grass
And a Green Chill upon the Heat
So ominous did pass
We barred the Windows and the Doors
As from an Emerald Ghost–
The Doom's electric Moccasin
That very instant passed–
On a strange Mob of panting Trees
And Fences fled away
And Rivers where the Houses ran
Those looked that lived–that Day–
The Bell within the steeple wild
The flying tidings told–

How much can come,
How much can go,
And yet abide the World!

Poems To Inspire Your Work:

LOVE POEM WITHOUT A DROP OF HYPERBOLE IN IT

I love you like ladybugs love windowsills, love you
like sperm whales love squid. There's no depth
I wouldn't follow you through. I love you like
the pawns in chess love aristocratic horses.
I'll throw myself in front of a bishop or a queen
for you. Even a sentient castle. My love is crazy
like that. I like that sweet little hothouse mouth
you have. I like to kiss you with tongue, with gusto,
with socks still on. I love you like a vulture loves
the careless deer at the roadside. I want to get
all up in you. I love you like Isis loved Osiris,
but her devotion came up a few inches short.
I'd train my breath and learn to read sonar until
I retrieved every lost blood vessel of you. I swear
this love is ungodly, not an ounce of suffering in it.
Like salmon and its upstream itch, I'll dodge grizzlies
for you. Like hawks and skyscraper rooftops,
I'll keep coming back. Maddened. A little hopeless.
Embarrassingly in love. And that's why I'm on
the couch kissing pictures on my phone instead of
calling you in from the kitchen where you are
undoubtedly making dinner too spicy, but when
you hold the spoon to my lips and ask if it's ready
I'll say it is, always, but never, there is never enough.

by Traci Brimhall

SHOES LIKE SNOW

He thinks he might have met her in a bank.
She's the kind who prattles (I met this guy . . .),

leaves her wooden window, hides in the safe
counting dimes. The other tellers hate her.

When he, his check and deposit slip arrive
$68.85, she says out loud: $68.85.

Or she's the kind who slides what he'd never buy
on his feet warm from high-tops: wing-tipped Florsheims.

How do they feel, she asks. He walks around, stops
in every mirror, slanted, knee-high. Rubs his neck,

preoccupied. Wants to see her shoehorn, ease her into every shoe
in stock, help her find the mates to all the ones abandoned

on Route 9. And she follows. They stand in traffic, ask each driver
idling at the light: Where are the shoes? When are they coming back?

The drivers think they want to wash their windshields,
attempt to buy them away with dollar bills. What does it mean

to wait for the other shoe to drop they ask the housewife, lawyer,
the guy driving Hugh's Appliance Truck. It starts snowing

shoes, tongues they haven't seen since childhood. He thinks
they might have met in Torrance, he might have known

the sewer grate she and Crystal Asmar sat atop on humid
afternoons, he might have been among the ones she chased,

she might have found him spinning like the teacher asked,
in Thrifty where the food was cheap, in the Pacific.

And the weather bears them leather uppers, spiked heels,
rubber soles, heavy accumulations, not one pair unmatched.

by Martha Silano

Chapter 28: Looking At All Sides

An old saying exists about a couple in a rocky relationship: "There are three sides to every story: his, hers, and the truth." An undone relationship isn't the only instance or circumstance that comes under scrutiny. The list of "the good, the bad, and the truth" focuses on subjects such as being single, adoption, working for oneself, indexed annuities, weight training, and food of every kind, to name a few.

Truth is indisputable. According to Dictionary.com, it is "the true or actual state of a matter." Truth is dependent on facts, standards, authenticity. Truth conforms to fact or reality, such as mathematical truths.

The opposite of truth is false or falsehood, which means untrue or deceptive. According to Dictionary.com, falsehood means "a lie; fiction; an untrue idea or belief; lack of conformity to truth or fact."

I learned, working as a reporter, that when I asked two or four or five people at an accident scene what had happened, I received responses that differed in some way from the other accounts. Those witnesses weren't lying. They weren't attempting to be deceptive. They just saw things differently. This is because we interpret and remember things based on who we are. In the studies of mass communication, the Consistency Theory explains that we respond to media based on who we are, where we came from, how we were raised, etc.

Exercise 1: The Naked Truth

Write a poem about the "naked truth." Think about a mistake you made or a lie you told, large or small. Highlight what prompted you to make this mistake or tell this lie. Did you know better? What were the repercussions? Did others forgive you? In your poem, show the bad in this situation, the hurt, the betrayal. Show no mercy as your write about your mistake/lie with blunt truthfulness.

Exercise 2: An Outright Lie

Write a poem about a lie that someone told you—a lie that you believed until you found out the truth. Who told you the lie? Why did he/she/they tell it? How upset were you once you found out the truth? How was "the truth" revealed? Did you feel betrayed? Were you able to forgive this person? As a twist for this poem, focus on the good in this situation, the lesson, what you learned. Maybe your child told you a lie because, in some circumstances, you are unapproachable and easily angered. Perhaps your child lying to you taught you to be more understanding and patient. Find the positive.

Exercise 3: Perspective—His, Hers, Their, And The Dog's

Write a poem about an event involving two people from the perspective of one of the participants. The topic could be an argument, a romantic moment, an accident, the viewing of something spectacular, an experience in nature, a disagreement at a restaurant, etc.

Now, rewrite the poem from the perspective of the other person who is involved. Try to enter into his/her/their mind and capture how his/her/their perspective might differ.

Once you have completed the second perspective, rewrite the poem from the perspective of an observer. Use a surprise observer, such as a bird, dog, waiter, neighbor, etc. For instance, use the bird's voice as it looks down from a tree branch on a married couple in a heated argument. What would it look like and sound like to the bird? Imagine a waiter overhearing an argument between a mom and a teenage daughter during lunch.

Poems To Inspire Your Work:

STANDING ON THE CORNER WHEN BEING COOL WENT BLIND
You've been slipping into darkness, whoa-whoa-whoa,
And pretty soon you're gonna pay.
    – War

Yeah baby, I'm the bushman, everybody know me, a talking
drum, I am the oral tradition, the griot of the cigarette. No
bullshit. Ain't nothing but the truth, everything I tell you
is airtight and waterproof. I can hoodoo and close view this
neighborhood's future from the vantage of my stoop. Get down
like I'm proud. I like mud-cloth so let that be my sanctified
robe. Preach asked me what my religion was and I told him
I channeled John Coltrane and became a devout musician. I
always been a child of god, if you don't believe me just ask my

blessed beloved mom. But tell me why do god's children have to experience every test? And exactly how much of a blessing comes with a financial offering? Well, consider the fact that all our damned deeds need to be sermonized and somewhere deep in that sin darkness there's always a crack of light. It ain't for sale but nothing in this world is half-priced, and if what you end up with does not satisfy nobody's giving you that money back. Can you see me in that light, with the children of god, those blues people with the haints riding them hard. Please do tell all the other infidels that I believe the choruses falling out the mouths of the raggedy people that I'm around are the actual utterances of saints.

by Gary Copeland Lilley

ರಾ

HUAQUEROS
Inca Pisac, Peru

Across the ravine from the ruins, holes
they gouged in a hillside—
hundreds of them, in rows—
resemble a woodpecker's industry.

Adobe bricks litter the slope, remains
of walls they chiseled away.
Each tomb, once broken, in a single breath
bled out a spirit and was void.

They extracted the skeleton that rested
in fetal position.
Then, with flashlights, probes of steel rods,
their search for *huaca*, the sacred

thing: a woven mantle,
a point-bottom pot for corn beer,
a llama figurine cast in gold.
I picture myself walking into Greenwood,

bouquet in hand, approaching the grave
of my mother, dead these two years,
finding dirt in a pile again,
shards of her clay urn.

Quechua poor dislodge their ancient
ancestors, loot the tombs
to feed their families.
They fuel traffic

bound for the gallery, the museum case,
the wall niche in a sunken
living room: *It looks just
as though it belongs there, don't you think?*

by John Willson

࿓

DANCE OF THE PRESIDENTIAL DEBATE

Ahh the fox-trot of words
and footwork of phrases
before the strut-your-stuff
breakdown and the shimmy—
shimmy turns into a mosh pit,
a twist and twerk, consonants
cutting across the podiums,
vowels caught in a pirouette
of syllables, a dipthong cha-cha-cha
not a pas de deux of ideas
but a war dance where tongues
and speech organs groan,
a dirty dance so one candidate
will do the country's frug
and jive us to prosperity.

by John Davis

Chapter 29: Follow Your Nose

In *A Natural History of the Senses*, Diane Ackerman writes, "Our cerebral hemispheres were originally buds from the olfactory stalks. We think because we smelled." Amazing. According to *Journal*, humans can discriminate at least one trillion olfactory stimuli (smells).

Here are a few more interesting facts about smell:

—Smell is the oldest sense.
—Your sense of smell goes directly to your brain.
—Women have a better sense of smell than men.
—Each person has his or her or their own distinct odor.
—The smell of sweat used to be exotic.

Chip Hanlon in an article titled "Writing With Your Nose" states, "So why do so few of them (reporters) take advantage of that olfactory skill in their writing?" Why does any writer not use that sense as much as the others? Especially because smells trigger memories more quickly than the other senses—because smells are like the nighthawk you can't see in the dark, like being so caught up in a visual, tactile, and sound-filled world we forget to breathe.

Exercise 1: The Crescent Moon Smells Like...

To begin this exercise, read through the following list of smells. If you like, add other smells to this list:

acrid, citrusy, cool, coppery, musty, pungent, putrid, rancid, rotten, salty, sour, spicy, stale, woody, yeasty, etc.

Now, write a poem using as many of the smells from this list (and the ones you may have added) as you can. Begin your poem with something that you normally wouldn't think of in terms of smell, such as fresh fallen snow, a night with no moon, a glass of water, or sunlight and give this image a certain smell. From there, continue to add interesting images and corresponding smells.

Exercise 2: Curry, Ginger, and Cinnamon

Choose a smell and write a poem using images, thoughts, and memories associated with a certain scent from your childhood and/or your culture–perhaps the smell of chickens in your grandmother's backyard, the smell of curry in a pot on the stove, refried beans being made in your aunt's kitchen, incense, Lysol, perfume, cologne, kerosene, hyacinths, coal, bleached sheets drying on the line, a cedar chest, or jail cell. Use specific details to help your reader enter into the aroma experience of your poem.

Poems To Inspire Your Work:

REGARDING THE ABSENT HEAT OF YOUR SKIN ON LETTERS
   I RECEIVE WHILE AT SEA

Paper wing   Words smudged
in your hand's stroke   What
has been sealed   Torn mouth

Lung-must

And a shiver along
my lateral line, olfactory
lobe lit up

Breath on the paper
Wind on the water (& off it)
Breath from the water
And ill wind   Tear-salt

Fish near the surface, glinting
Plankton rising   forced

Scent of panic   (lung-must)
Petrels arrive because of
Patter and feed

Your eyes on the horizon
are greedy, could eat
leagues   Call my name

Breeze   Wind   Gale
Let the air clock around your mouth

It pushes, unturned,
against your mouth

If you stand on the shore and call
I'll know

by Elizabeth Bradfield

೮ಂ

SCENTED APE DANCING IN THE GARDEN

He will know you by your sweat,
my grandmother says. *This has been*
our way long as anyone remembers.
Under my right armpit, I lodge
the slice of a red-skinned apple.

My feet follow accordion and violin,
the touch of this one's fingers,
then the next, dance after dance
until I meet him, the one I know
whose mouth wants to meet my lips
and suckle my breasts.

I hand him the slice, and as
the sweet juice of me runs down
his throat, I see he wants to come
into my garden.

by Susan Landgraf

೮ಂ

INSTEAD OF DEATH I CHOOSE

to plan for tomorrow's tomorrow
buy a new planner and even scribble deadlines
I swoon at the daphne odoras
scent that rides dusk winds
delivers hope to my naked nose.

Instead of urine soaked folds of skin
needles strewn at your feet, eyes vacant, body rotting
cracked chairs thrown toward red-lighted cars
I choose to remember you are someone's son
and I am someone's mother.

Instead of accepting the rich richer
shipping overnight packages breaking backs
displacing profits the rest of us fail to realize
I choose to peruse the farmer's market
locals nourishing locals.

Instead of fear I choose
to sit with silenced silences
a thousand missed connections, missed
engagements never made.
I approach you old friend with new bravery.

by Kathryn Thurber-Smith

Chapter 30: Leave No Stone Unturned

Think about the differences in stones and the places where they're found: stones falling on a casket as it's being buried, stones in your shoe, a stone speckled with rain, a stone polished by waves, stones pushed up from below by a mole or gopher, stones thrown from erupting volcanoes, stones stacked on one another to create fences, stones falling to earth in the form of meteorites. The ground is always birthing stones. Stones hold up the world.

Exercise 1: What The Stone Says

Go out and find a stone. Meditate on that stone—how it was born, how it came to be in this world above ground. What does it remember about its deep, deep below-ground existence before being birthed out of fire? Let it speak to you as you contemplate its story. Be imaginative as you let your stone speak. Write a poem that:

- —traces the stone's journey from its birth to the place where you found it
- —talks about its importance in the world; what the stone's "job" is
- —compares the stone to something else, like a tree, an animal, a mountain, etc.

Exercise 2: Wise As A Stone

Think about the stone you have found as being a messenger delivering important news or words of wisdom to the world. Maybe your stone has something to say about climate change, the current state of politics, the entertainment industry, the future of space exploration, how to save endangered species, how to achieve lasting world peace, etc. Try to imagine the stone's perspective—what would a stone really "think" about climate change, especially if that stone had been carried for thousands of years and hundreds of miles in a glacier during an ice age?

Exercise 3: Speak Of The Stone

Write a poem in which you invent a new saying or adage that uses the word stone(s), like "The stone is mightier than the sword," substituting "stone" for "pen" or "The road to hell is paved with good stones," substituting "stones" for "intentions, or "The best things in life are stones," substituting "stones" for "free."

Here are a few sayings to have fun with:

> A penny for your thoughts
> Barking up the wrong tree
> Once in a blue moon
> Don't put all your eggs in one basket
> Don't let the cat out of the bag
> It's a piece of cake
> A picture paints a thousand words
> At the drop of a hat
> That's the last straw
> Speak of the devil
> Actions speak louder than words

Poems To Inspire Your Work:

STONE

You loosened easier than your smaller, meaner kin,
though not without help from a sturdy stick.
Now, washed and dried and studied for your
scars and speckles, you sit before me.

Gray fontanel: baby alien.
Oval: prehistoric egg that failed to hatch
its lumbering beast.
Rusty fringe: man caught midlife, balding.

But you are none of these.
You are what you said when I pried you
from the hard dirt.
Hold me, you said, and I will give you heft.
Hold me and know how straight you stand.
Feel your confident stride?
Hold me and go forth.

With me in hand, we will slay giants.

by Lynn Knight

&

A STONE ON THE ROAD

becomes a body, becomes a rag.
This is how it happens. Once

I sorted through possessions on the floor
of the living room: newspaper, coffee cup

cat toy, dead rat. It was dark. My hand
grasped the soft body, rejected its spentness,

death tangible, limp. One can use a rag
over and over and over

until it wears thin, until it gives
out, sieves what we most want

to disappear.
A father can be like that.

He can breathe and talk and eat
and worry and worry and worry

until he's eaten from the inside out.
Until he is ragged. A stone in pocket.

by Ronda Piszk Broatch

Chapter 31: Who or What Is Your Muse?

A muse is often defined as the person (or thing) who inspires creativity in an artist. For instance, the photographer Dora Maar was a muse for Picasso; President Kennedy's daughter, Caroline, was a muse for singer/songwriter Neil Diamond; Diego Rivera was often a muse for Frida Kahlo; Tom Lefroy, who courted Jane Austen, was a muse for many of her novels. Henry David Thoreau's muse was nature, especially the forest; Claude Monet's muse was flower gardens; Herman Melville's muse was the ocean. Andy Warhol's muse was often his beloved dog, Archie, and Salvador Dali sometimes considered cats his muse.

The term "muse" has its origin in Greek mythology in the story of the nine daughters (nine muses) born of Mnemosyne and Zeus, in a union "of divine love." Each daughter (muse) is charged with being the inspiration behind the following fields of art and science:

> Calliope: Muse of heroic and epic poetry, storytelling and eloquence of speech
> Clio: Muse of history and writing, and giver of fame
> Erato: Muse of Eros, desire and love poetry
> Euterpe: Muse of music and bringer of joy
> Terpsichore: Muse of dance and movement
> Thalia: Muse of comedy, play, and celebration
> Polyhymnia: Muse of sacred hymns, poetry, and oration
> Melpomene: Muse of tragedy who opens the heart through grieving
> Urania: Muse of astronomy and science

Take a moment to think about who and/or what inspires you in your creative activities. You might find that you have several muses, depending on what activity or project you are doing. Maybe if you love to cook, your muse is Julia Child as you make dinner, but when you sit down later to write a poem, you find that looking out your window into the vastness of space and stars is your muse. Perhaps your muse is an ex-boyfriend/girlfriend whom you have never stopped loving, your long-time pet, a certain celebrity, a teacher, a famous writer/poet, or the seashore. Think about who and what causes the spark of creativity to light within you.

Exercise 1: Help Me, Thalia

Study the Greek muses in the list above. Choose a muse and her field of inspiration and write a poem based on your choice. For instance, if you pick Thalia (muse of comedy, play, and celebration), write a poem that calls on Thalia to help you in her particular fields. Perhaps your body and mind are both in need of a day, or at least several hours, of down time or play. Make a list of things you could do: Watch five stand-up comedy shows on Netflix, go outside and play on some swings, rent a rowboat and have fun in the water, plan a huge party, overindulge and enjoy some of your favorite foods, etc. Choose one or more of your Thalia-inspired items to use in your poem.

If, on the other hand, you choose Euterpe (muse of music and bringer of joy), consider writing your poem as you listen to some of your favorite songs or classical composers. Sing or hum as you write. Allow some of the lyrics to infuse your poem. If you are listening to the Beatles' classic "Revolution" maybe a few partial lines might appear in your poem, such as "it's evolution," "you can count me out," "you have to wait," "it's gonna be all right," "change the constitution," etc. In your poem, you might call on Euterpe to bring harmony to your life or help you learn a musical instrument or maybe she will inspire a memory of a certain song that reminds you of an embarrassing eighth grade dance. Let music flow through your writing.

Exercise 2: Thank You, Sylvia

Write down your muses (people, things, animals, locations in the natural world, cities, etc.) in terms of your creative activities—writing, cooking, painting, making music, designing clothing, gardening, playing a certain sport, acting, dancing, sculpting, etc. Maybe your muse(s) is deceased or a person/animal that is currently in your life. Maybe your muse is Paris or a wildlife refuge for birds or your grandmother's favorite locket that you now own. Maybe Sylvia Plath is your muse when you write poetry, but Marta is your muse when you play soccer every Saturday. Write a poem that celebrates the person/animal/place/thing that inspires you (you can mention more than one). If Frida Kahlo inspires you when you dabble in visual art, write a poem that honors everything about Frida that helps you dive into your watercolors and create something breathtaking on the canvas.

Poems To Inspire Your Work:

VIVA LA VIDA
I will look down on you from all the corners of the earth.
  – Frida Kahlo

We keep you close in
            silver, jade, and coral –
around wrists, the base

of throats, where pulses
            rush under your brazen gaze.
You hang from our lobes –

whispering reminders to speak with
            truth's switchblade tongue, a mouth-
ful of blood better than self-betrayal.

We slide your courage onto
            fingers so when we stroke new lovers
the body's yearning outshines

white corsets and braced bones.
            We cannot forget your stranded
days in the bed of the Blue House,

your black hair wreathed with flowers,
            swept high into braids wild as vines.
Even in the slipping

away, you painted
            VIVA LA VIDA
in red oil across

the sweet flesh
            of watermelon
riddled with seeds.

by Kelly Cressio-Moeller

MUSE

In my youth's years, she loved me, I am sure.
The flute of seven pipes she gave in my tenure
And harked to me with smile—without speed,
Along the ringing holes of the reed,
I got to play with my non-artful fingers
The peaceful songs of Phrygian village singers,
And the important hymns, that gods to mortals bade.
From morn till night in oaks' silent shade
I diligently harked to the mysterious virgin;
Rewarding me, by chance, for any good decision,
And taking locks aside of the enchanting face,
She sometimes took from me the flute, such commonplace.
The reed became alive in consecrated breathing
And filled the heart with holiness unceasing.

by Alexander Sergeyevich Pushkin

SOLUTION (an excerpt)

I am the Muse who sung alway
By Jove, at dawn of the first day.
Star-crowned, sole-sitting, long I wrought
To fire the stagnant earth with thought:
On spawning slime my song prevails,
Wolves shed their fangs, and dragons scales;
Flushed in the sky the sweet May-morn,
Earth smiled with flowers, and man was born.
Then Asia yeaned her shepherd race,
And Nile substructs her granite base, —
Tented Tartary, columned Nile, —
And, under vines, on rocky isle,
Or on wind-blown sea-marge bleak,
Forward stepped the perfect Greek:

That wit and joy might find a tongue,
And earth grow civil, HOMER Sung.

Flown to Italy from Greece,
I brooded long, and held my peace,
For I am wont to sing uncalled,
And in days of evil plight
Unlock doors of new delight;
And sometimes mankind I appalled
With a bitter horoscope,
With spasms of terror for balm of hope.
Then by better thought I lead
Bards to speak what nations need;
So I folded me in fears,
And DANTE searched the triple spheres,
Moulding nature at his will,
So shaped, so coloured, swift or still,
And, sculptor-like, his large design
Etched on Alp and Apennine…

by Ralph Waldo Emerson

Chapter 32: The Poet and The Sea

Perhaps no other place on our planet inspires writers and artists like the sea. Consider these facts about our oceans:

—More than two million species of plants and animals live in the ocean.
—Scientists estimate that millions of species are still undiscovered in the ocean.
—80% of all life on earth can be found in the ocean.
—Ocean plants produce half of the oxygen in our atmosphere.
—3.5 billion people rely on the ocean as a food source.
—One in every six jobs is marine related.
—The ocean covers 70% of the earth's surface.

Below is a small list of species that live in the ocean. Taste these words. Say these words aloud very slowly and savor the sounds. Allow your imagination to conjure images of these living things (even if you don't know what they look like.) What do their names inspire your imagination to create?. Spend some time going over this list at least twice:

sea anemone, jellyfish, starfish, oyster, salmon, ribbon worm, burrowing sea cucumber, sea slug, sea urchin, cephalopod, scallop, mussel, chambered nautilus, dolphin, shark, whale, frosted nudibranch, sea lemon, moon jelly, stalked hairy sea squirt, Dungeness crab, coon strip shrimp, geoduck, mossy chiton, big skate, red Irish lord, quillback rockfish, painted greenling, pile perch, mosshead warbonnet, penpoint gunnel, plainfin midshipman, norther spearnose poacher, tube snout, bay pipe fish, blood seastar, scalyhead sculpin, shiny orange sea squirt

This list is only the tip of the iceberg. For those of us who live around water, we know some of these creatures. Perhaps we went out and dug clams or fished for perch or went scuba diving, or maybe we felt the wetness and smell, that smell that only the sea brings—algae, salt, whatever the sea can drag up on the beaches–from beer bottles to syringes, dead seal pups to glass floats, oddly shaped driftwood to tiny hermit crabs.

People who live close to the sea get close and personal with words such as:

filamentous, gelatinous, luminescent, diatoms, tentacles, spirals, siphons, whorls, suckers, calcareous spicules, siliceous spicules, polyps, pipes, lappets, medusae, carapaces, tentacles, bowls, glassy aggregates, suckerlike tips, drill-shaped, coiled, conical, valved, hinged

Some say that at the beginning of the earth's birth, earth was one big sea. And we, as humans, are mostly water–55-78% of our body weight. The sea giveth and the sea taketh. It took my stepsister and it almost took me. I am afraid of the sea (of water in general, except for a bath or shower), but I'm also drawn to it–its mystery, life-giving force, the creatures from the sea I eat: lobster, prawns, mussels, oysters, rockfish.

Exercise 1: Tentacles And Picnics

What experiences have you had with the sea? Have you been afraid? In awe? Did you love getting sand in your toes, sand in your shoes? Or did you want a shower after walking on the beach? Did the smell of the salt air and walking into a strong wind make you feel more alive? Or did it bother you? And if you have never had the opportunity to visit an ocean beach, what intrigues you most about the ocean? How do you imagine what salt air will feel like in your nose, mouth, lungs? Will you stand back and watch the waves or will you run into the water so that your skin can directly experience it? What beach would you like to visit first?

Write a poem making use of some of your favorite words at the beginning of this exercise—if you love the sound of a word, but you aren't sure what it means, such as "chiton" or "lappet," look it up in an online dictionary. Mix these wonderful words with your memories and experiences of the sea or with your dreams of one day visiting the ocean. You may end up with a poem that combines a surfing wipeout with red Irish lord, scalyhead sculpin, whorls, and tentacles. Mix a fond memory of a picnic in the sand with moon jelly, gelatinous, and stalked hairy sea squirt.

Exercise 2: Swishing And Swashing

The following is a list of sea sounds. Feel free to add your own words to this group:

swish swash/swash swish, flip flap, slap slap, plip plop, plink plank, gurgle, fin fan, smack, plunk, burble, click, trill, whistle, thump, moan, groan, growl, grunt, squeak, rasp, rap, hiss, drum, puff, stick-slip, rumble, crack

Using some of the above sea-sound words, write a poem in which you find something on the beach. This "something" can be an expected beach item: shell, agate, dead fish, seagull feather, a sandal, a fast food cup, a scurrying crab, etc. Or, this item could be something a little more fanciful and imaginative: a key to a treasure chest, a diamond ring, a note in a bottle, a pirate sword, a wooden leg, a mermaid who asks for your help, etc. Be creative with this poem and don't be afraid to venture into the realm of the surreal. Maybe you find a potion in the sand that allows you to suddenly sprout gills, and you take off on an undersea adventure. If you want to get really wild in this poem, consider beginning it, "In the dream, I suddenly found myself..." And, don't forget to use your sea-sounds.

Poems To Inspire Your Work:

AT THE FOULWEATHER BLUFF PRESERVE

Ground fog hangs over the water
of Puget Sound as we emerge
out of alders to advance on the beach.
The two-prong tracks of deer
lie before us like stringed beads leading
away. Our sneakers skitter on slippery
stones, eyes examining the sea wrack
tangled from tidal zones: oyster shells
fused together, cockle shells that shatter
like china plates beneath our weight,
skeletons of sand dollars smaller than nickels.

          The stiller we stand,
the more we can see—so many baby white crabs.
Then a clatter, a rattling trill, and a kingfisher
dives low, warning us. The returning tide
freshens anemones and colonies of clams
as the sky clears to blue so bright,
we shade our eyes with hands scratched by sand,
full of what the sea has left behind.

by Sharon Hashimoto

CAPILLARY ACTION
— for Arctic Explorer Donald B. MacMillan

A straw, a string lowered
into surface
tension
and the liquid climbs as far as it can.

Consider our ring of latitude, Mac,
(your Gulf of Maine, my Puget Sound)
as water settled to its level
in the globe's great bowl.

The coasts are a thread
pinched above us at the pole.
We can't help being drawn.

Tears are pulled this way,
ducts glazing the eye.
O *Lacrymosa*,

said Mozart, giving in.
Sentiment, passion, biological lube—
all equip us to squint north.

by Elizabeth Bradfield

☙

LOW-/TIDE HEART OF MINE

That long-gone summer when I stood upright

on my board and paddled around the tide pools

at Short Beach, above the hermit crabs

scuttling over purple rocks looking for new

homes, below the planes landing, coming

back, so low I could see their metal bellies,

I cut through the hot solstice air, my balance

steady enough I could look over my tan shoulder,

back to the beach: kids, some crying, a small dog

chased a gull fat with fried food, and I think now

I was happy, or if not happy, nothing fed this low-

tide heart of mine. I remember it was mid-

year and I had yet to give back even an inch of light.

by Jennifer Martelli

Chapter 33: Sounding Life into Your Poems

Sounds slice the air, break barriers—and hold the world together. What about our poems? Where's the sound? Where's that poem that blows, whispers, or tap dances across the Olympic Mountains? Or maybe it huffs, grunts, and farts its way. Don Maxwell wrote, "Even a great poem on a *page* isn't poetry. You have to get it *off* the page and into the air to make it poetry. You have to *say* it to make it poetry." There are millions of voices over many centuries, and all poems rest on sound—the sound of words, the rhythm of words, the meaning of words and the new meaning that comes when all the parts of a poem are singing in perfect key. Sound happens in so many ways. All of the following come into play. You might know them, but here's a review:

Alliteration: the beginning letters or repetition of initial sounds (usually consonants) of two or more words are the same. Examples: "Peter Piper picked a peck..." or "Some summer soon she..."

Assonance: the same or similar vowel sounds – pie and pipe, home and loan, knife and night.

Cacophony: discordant, jarring sounds – lightning spat, cackled, cracked the stones.

Caesura: a pause or break in the middle of a line using a dash or comma or period.

Consonance: sounds in agreement with tone; repetition of the same end consonants where the stressed syllables agree: black and brick, road and cold, window and syndrome.

End-stopped line: each line has a logical close at its end, usually with a period or semicolon.

Enjambment: a line that breaks before the end of a sentence.

Free verse: makes use of such devices as repetition of words and phrases, breath units, assonance, consonance, alliteration.

Metrical verse: formal verse with a system of stressed and unstressed syllables (known as feet, with the same number of feet in each line throughout the poem); formal verse makes use of a pattern of rhymed endings.

Onomatopoeia: the words sound like the object or idea–sizzle, bang, pop.

Repetition: repeating the same word or phrase for a particular effect.

Exact rhyme: full or perfect rhyme – sold and bold, king and wing, whisper and blister.

Slant or near rhyme: half or imperfect rhyme – stone and moon, yellow and shallow.

Internal rhyme: rhyme within the line.

End rhyme: rhyme at the end of the line.

Stressed or end-stop ending: stressed syllable comes at the end of the line– remorse, stored, syringe, talk.

Unstressed or falling ending: unstressed syllable comes at the end of the line– cherries, migraine, remember.

Exercise 1: Consonance Rant

Write a poem using words that demonstrate the concept of consonance such as *click, clunk, scrape, prick, track, peck, poke, cackle*. If you would like, add more words with the "ck" sound to this list. Your poem can have any topic, but because these sounds tend to be harsh, loud, or even angry sounding, consider writing a "rant" poem about something that is upsetting to you— personally, politically, globally, etc.

Exercise 2: A Line With Internal Rhyme

Write a poem that uses internal rhyme—rhymes that occur within a line, not at the end. Before you begin, create a list of paired rhymes and draw from these words as you compose your poem. Here is a list to help you begin:

>   long /wrong
>   barricade /marinade
>   blue /shoe /flew
>   make / break
>   group / soup

sleep / creep
line / rhyme

A <u>line</u> with internal <u>rhyme</u> might look something like this sentence.

Consider writing your poem about a recent event that you have experienced which left you feeling confused or amused.

Exercise 3: The "Aaaaa" Moments

Vowel sounds can create emotion in a poem—the "aaaaa" and the "ooooo" moments of life. Write a poem using assonance about an experience you've had that caused you to feel intense awe or a sense of something profound—birth, an incredible nature scene, a sudden insight about life, an epiphany moment where something troubling you becomes clear, a deep relationship, etc. Make sure to use words thick with vowel sounds, particularly words with "aa" and "oo" sounds like "moon," "tune," "balloon," "ash," "blast," "glasses," etc.

Exercise 4: Honk If You Love Bruises

Choose ten words that are unpleasant and ugly sounding (in your ear or to your eye)—bruise, maggot, exhaust, moist, phlegm, honk, crotch, curdle, scab, gut, butt, chunky, etc.—and write a happy, light-hearted poem. Note how using these "ugly" words keeps your poem from becoming overly sentimental. Think about how you can incorporate unpleasant words into a beautiful nature scene or how you can include them in a love poem.

Poems To Inspire Your Work:

FOUR NIGHTS IN THE MISTY FJORDS

She was inside the whalebone
counting the looped ritual
that followed her below deck.
She was the smell of crayfish
and crab, cracking them open,
tearing out their sweet meat.
This is what she did when the shells

split. She kept them until they dried
inside like a gull's white dung.
She layered the hours with it —
when everyone lay in their bunks
and the stars were hammers on the sea.
She could feel their weight — hear
the surrender of the old halibut
before the hook found passage.
Blackwater pulling on a line,
pulling like the night, creaking
like a lie. And when she closed her eyes
and her body sank down
that's when he would appear, cinch
in his hand, twisting the anchor
until it snapped, watching her drop
in the dark. The rope unraveling
from the rust so swiftly, it burned
to touch. Nothing but nightfall
at the river's mouth and the slow
motion of salmon waiting to be caught.

by Lois P. Jones

⁂

NOT THE STARS

A rumble of cars and conversations
rustled like papyrus, when suddenly the tall

buildings gather around me like the walls
of a well, and bright in the shred of sky

the stars. Tall flags barely fluttered,
the talk and traffic shuffled on.

And behind them a sound
like breathing, not anyone's. Huge,

as if the day had lungs. Not to be
believed, but there it was, and what it was

didn't matter as long as it went on
filling and emptying and not our own.

by Robert McNamara

℘

ALONE, THEY SPEAK

Cattails
avening, hoosh, hoosh
next to the highway

Oranges
suns in their sections singing
their slippers of song

Rain
crystal mouths calling
to the birch boughs
like clear-bellied bells

Periwinkles
blue blue out of the magician's brew
the earth sighing full, my child, full

Sunset
swathing the end of the day, ready
for her sister on the other side

Morning
moon whish moon whish and hums
and strums and whooshes

Highway
black snake swish swath
through the fields ohree ohree

The River
a curve of ripples, rapids and a bend
Ohming to itself: ohm ohm ohm

by Susan Landgraf

Chapter 34: Women's Voices in the World

We write from the cultural influences of our place—towns, regions, countries—and our voices capture the unique landscape, philosophy, history and personal narratives that we come from. Yet there are common denominators that we all share regardless of our backgrounds.

Exercise 1: Inspired By Titles

Look over the list below of titles of poems written by seven women poets from around the world. Titles of poems (and collections) can pack a lot of power. What themes can you associate with each of these women by a few titles? Love? Fear? Loss? Freedom? Motherhood?

Choose at least three titles from the list below and write the words you associate with each title—memories, what you know about the meanings of the words, the emotion the poem title evokes in you, the images that arise, etc.

For instance, if you chose "Arabian Nights" by Nimah Ismail Nawwab, you might generate a list such as this:

> intrigue
> Aladdin
> Ali Baba
> purple
> gold
> peacock
> stars
> darkness
> magic carpet
> bangles

Now write a poem using those words. See where it takes you. For example:

Words crowded my mouth:
Aladdin. Ali Baba. Peacocks.
I wanted in
to that purple and gold world,
the dark sky lit with the flash
of my gold bangles...

Here is a list of women poets and titles (bios appear between Exercise 1 & 2):

Gwendolyn Brooks:

"Sadie and Maud"
"The Bean Eaters"
"We Real Cool"

Carol Ann Duffy:

"If I Was Dead"
"The Bees"
"Whoever She Was"

Gabriela Mistral:

"I am Not Alone"
"The Sad Mother"
"Those Who Do Not Dance"

Nimah Ismail Nawwab:

"Arabian Nights"
"Banishment"
"Nightmare"

Amrita Pritam:

"A Needle of Light"
"The First Creation"
"The Virgin"

Naomi Shihab Nye:

"Blood"
"Hidden"
"Making a Fist"

Lesya Ukrainka:

"Seven Strings"
"Smoke"
"The Forgotten Shadow"

Gwendolyn Brooks (US) attended four schools in Chicago, Illinois, which gave her a perspective on racial dynamics in the city. Born in 1917, she was appointed Poet Laureate of Illinois in 1968 and Poet Laureate Consultant in Poetry to the Library of Congress in 1985. The recipient of many honors, including a Guggenheim, she was the author of more than 20 books, including *Blacks*, *The Bean Eaters*, and *Annie Allen*, for which she received the Pulitzer Prize.

Carol Ann Duffy (Scotland) is a Scottish poet and playwright; she was appointed Britain's Poet Laureate in 2009. She won the T S Eliot Prize and the PEN/Pinter Prize, among many other prizes and awards.

Gabriela Mistral (Chile) was born in Vicuña, Chile. She taught school for many years and Spanish literature at a number of institutions, including Columbia University and the University of Puerto Rico. She served as the Chilean consul in Naples, Madrid, and Lisbon and was awarded the Nobel Prize for Literature in 1945; her complete poetry was published in 1958.

Nimah Ismail Nawwab (Saudi Arabia) is a Saudi poet, essayist, editor, and photographer, whose life is deeply rooted in the Arab world. Stephen L. Brundage of *Arab News* says that (Nimah speaks) "for the too-often silent voice of the Arab woman...a unique and articulate window to the soul." Her book *The Unfurling* became the fastest selling poetry book in the kingdom. Her work has been featured on BBC World News and Newsweek International.

Naomi Shihah Nye (US) was born in 1952 to a Palestinian father and American mother. The author of a number of poetry books, she has traveled for the United States Information Agency to promote international goodwill through the arts. She's received four Pushcart Prizes, a Guggenheim and the Academy of American Poets' Lavan Award. Her poems focus on roots, a sense of place (from St. Louis, Missouri, to Jerusalem and San Antonio, Texas), and similarities and differences between cultures.

Amrita Pritam (India) was born in 1919 in Gujranwala, a part of India that later became Pakistan. In 1947 she began to write in Hindi instead of her native language Punjabi. She was considered the first prominent woman Punjabi poet, novelist, and essayist and received India's highest literary award, the Bhartiya Jnanpith Award, in 1982. She also was awarded the Padma Vibhushan and was honored with India's highest literary award, the Sahitya Akademi Fellowship, given to the "immortals of literature."

Lesya Ukrainka (Ukraine), a poet, translator, and dramatist, was also a political, civil, and feminist activist. She wrote in Russian and Ukrainian. Considered one of the Ukraine's best known poets and writers, there are many monuments to her honor.

Exercise 2: Inspired By Lines

Below you will find some lines of poetry taken from Gwendolyn Brooks, Gabriela Mistral, Nimah Ismail Nawwab, Naomi Shihab Nye, and Amrita Pritam. Read over these lines slowly and consider reading them aloud. Ask yourself: What is similar about each poet? What makes each poet's voice unique? Which of these lines speak to you?

Choose a line from each poet and randomly create a five line "poem." For example:

how shall I dance
on a ripe line of sky
night-black lace
her scarf
slipped

Rewrite each line (and feel free to move the lines around as you compose) in order to create a unique five line poem inspired by these five women poets. The above lines might be changed to something like:

I remember we danced
on the balcony—a yellow skyline
I wore a black thrift-store dress and a scarf
you tugged until the scarf
fell at your feet

And, don't feel that you have to limit your poem to five lines. If you are inspired, keep writing. You can also incorporate more lines from below to create a longer poem.

Listed below are your lines of poetry:

Gwendolyn Brooks:

night-black lace
the deep-brown middle-brown high-brown of it

as they lean over the beans in their rented back room

Gabriela Mistral:

if they could, the trees would lift you
she has planted cactus and alien grass
how shall I dance?

Nimah Ismail Nawwab:

overlooking mysterious labyrinths, winding walkways
her scarf slipped
grief I let you go

Naomi Shihab Nye:

the little sucked-in breath of air
on a ripe line of sky
I want to be famous in the way a pulley is famous

Amrita Pritam:

only a few poems fell out of the ash
it has the police's stamp on it
we found that dog's carcass in the middle of a room

Poems To Inspire Your Work:

BUELITA

In my eight year old world,
I am the moon
orbiting Buelita,
my favorite Abuela.

Hummingbird quick,
Buelita flits
pristine, precise, powerful.

Shepherd's me
through the bilingual maze.
Español y Ingles
spoken together or apart.

Buelita calls me Jamona,
her lil' ham.
My secret performances
for her eyes only.

At dinner, I dance in my chair
singing and clapping
uno y dos,
to cumbias y rancheras.

Later, we gopher the cedar closet.
Unearth 3 woven palm boxes
carried on Buelita's head
from Mexico.
Their sweet scent surrendered.

Yet, the aroma of copalli resin
welcomes us to
our season
to honor death
and the cycle of life.

Memories trigger tears of love.
¡Mira! ¡Las Calacas!
Wood sculpted skeletons smirk,
their happy afterlife
dancing & playing music
in joyful attire.

Buelita hides a new one for me each year.
Under the sofa? No.
On top of the chest of drawers? No.
Mirth dances across Buelita's face.

¡Aha! Inside the freezer,
¡La Catrina!
Elegant icon of protest,
wide plumed hat
frames her Grande Dame glow.

Dusk embraces us.
La Catrina & I snip
bunches of marmalade orange
& lemon yellow marigolds.

Scatter fragrant petals,
up the tiered altar.
¡Bienvenidos familia!
Welcome home family.

Delicate unveiling of our dead,
Don Jose y Dona Maria
in smiling wedding photos.
Graciela, our cousin
Cheshire Cat grinning at the camera.

Tamales, atole, mole,
sugar skulls, pan de muerto y agua
welcome their tired and hungry
souls home after their journey.

Copalli aromas,
Marigold perfumes intoxicate.
We whisper prayers,
blow kisses
to our dearly departed.

Buelita and I sing,
"Every day is a dance with death.
Live every day as if it were your last one."
Luminous moon beams.

by Catalina Marie Cantú

WHY SOME HUNGARIANS DREAM EQUATIONS AND NOTES

More musicians and mathematicians
than anywhere else: too many Martians, not enough
spaceships to take them back – the sudden exodus
like a great flock of herons
slipping through a blue lip in the sky.

The gypsy women's skirts unfurled
to red and purple flowers, and the men's voices
reverberated like echoes
in a well. Their stories
flickered around the campfire: how the abandoned

pocketed themselves from the sea and the moon's pull,
whirled to the hum a compass needle makes
in the dark. They used scales as metaphors.
Their long-handled cups held the moon.
They mixed with the natives.

Finding blue bloods now would be hard as going home
without a ship – but a thread holds
the magnetic resonance in their equations,
their songs throbbing
with a blue planetary hum.

by Susan Landgraf

∞

MARÍA SATURNINA SULTRY YEARNING

The way skin holds us in
arching thoughts
and dreams like rainbows
between brain and bone
ovaries like twin moons
in darkness hang

while the heart tugs
a blazing sun
o compass rose
sister divine
water our gardens
let intuition flourish
let the feminine thrive

by Claudia Castro Luna

Chapter 35: Connect The Dots

James Dickey wrote that in writing poetry, "Connections between things... exist... in ways that they never did before." What are these things? What are the things, which, put together in a poem, make a whole world?

First, you need a place. You need a container to hold things. Picture that place. William Carlos Williams' poem "The Red Wheelbarrow" happens on a farm. Concrete nouns such as chickens, a wheelbarrow, and rain put us there. In "Woodchucks" by Maxine Kumin, the poem takes place in her yard and garden. Again, words such as puddingstone, marigolds, broccoli shoots, and roses put us there. In the poem "Root Cellar" by Theodore Roethke, bulbs, crates, roots, manure, and dirt give us what we'd expect to find in a root cellar, along with certain smells.

These poems put us somewhere and give us the things that show us the place. They also, each one, have energy, not just because something is happening but because the verbs infuse each poem with movement:

> In his 16-word poem, Williams uses the verbs depends and glazed.

> Kumin uses shoehorned, turned, brought, said, lapsed, puffed, drew, and died.

> Roethke employs broke, dangled, drooped, and hung.

Each of the three poems depends on the details of the place and what is happening there, each has movement and some sort of order, and each poem has a mystery about it. There's an undercurrent between what is happening and the emotions both stated and not. And each poem is about something bigger: killing, death, love, longing.

> With Williams we see a cycle and a turn from the title "The Red Wheelbarrow" to "a red wheel / barrow." This shift turns the poem from a rainy farm afternoon into a place of death.

> Kumin talks about death in the first line: "Gassing the woodchucks didn't turn out right." She goes on to show the destruction of her garden: "They brought down the marigolds... beheading the carrots." We also see her conflicted emotions: "a lapsed pacifist" who was "righteously thrilling / to the feel of the .22."

Roethke sets up certainty in how he places us in his poem and a sense of danger; the fact that things we don't think about, such as dark shoots and stems, can be living lives that should give us pause, and that love and hate sometimes share the same bed.

Exercise 1: Focus On Location And Setting

Pick a place you know or once knew. The smaller the place, the better. For example:

—grandmother's kitchen
—first grade classroom
—first night in a jail cell
—a hotel in Baghdad
—the dentist's chair
—father's hospital room

Next, put things in that place. For example:

—stove, window, rolling pin, the smell of chicken soup bubbling in a pot
—bare lightbulb overhead, light between the bars, gasping sounds from the cell next door
—sink, tray covered with a white paper napkin, the sound of a drill in the next cubicle

Now, recall something that went wrong and hurt you in that particular place or something positive that happened. For example:

—burned your hand on the stove or the taste of warm cinnamon oatmeal cookies
—the smell of metal and urine and fear or your aunt showed up and bailed you out
—paper bib around your neck, dentist's big nose, and the cold metal instruments or you weren't berated for not flossing, and you had no cavities

Lastly, use all three of your elements in a poem: your specific place, the things in that place, and how you either had a negative or positive experience in that place (or both). Use surprising images, vivid descriptions, and active verbs. If you want, include a mysterious element in your poem—maybe in your grandmother's kitchen you felt as if your deceased grandfather were sitting at the table or maybe there was an odd stranger who shared a jail cell with you and he/she seemed otherworldly. Create a poem that takes your reader to your specific location so that he/she will leave your poem with a profound and lingering experience.

Exercise 2: A Sports Car In Oz

Write a quick response for each of the following words—a single word, a phrase—whatever comes to mind. Don't think or edit; just write.

> coffee cup
> hairbrush
> flag
> laptop computer
> teacher
> grass
> lightning
> cell phone
> knife
> rust
> sand
> birthday card
> bird
> sports car

Now, put two of these items in a place. It doesn't have to be a place you know or are familiar with. For example:

> —coffee cup and cell phone on the kitchen counter near the loaf of bread
> —your teacher and a flag in your fourth grade classroom
> —lightning and a bird in heaven or hell
> —a sports car and grass in Oz or at Hogwarts

Using your two items, the words you associate with them, and the particular place in which the items are found, write a poem that utilizes detailed images, concrete descriptions, and active verbs. Your poem can stay true to a certain memory you have (your teacher and flag in a specific classroom) or your poem can move into uncharted imagination (you and the Tin Man in a Tesla racing across a field of poppies looking for a witch). Try writing this poem in couplets and don't worry if it ends up being long and wordy.

Poems To Inspire Your Work:

AT THE SHELDON JACKSON MUSEUM

In the solemn glow
of amber light
and Plexiglas, silence
deep as arctic
winter, soft as sun
on birch, we move
from scene to scene
that show us how
they lived
until they perished
at the hands of Russian Traders
who stole their furs
and wives and left behind
their Christian God, Small Pox
and rot-gut whiskey burning
Third Avenue where they wander
bar to bar searching
for home. What was left
is in this careful
room: temperature
controlled, light subdued
on seal gut suits
luminous as skin, stitched
with sea grass, water tight
as kayaks strong enough
to carry men across
the swollen seas hunting
seal and whale.
Imagine small rooms
lit by oil light, fires burning,
women's laughter soft
as infants cooing, men
bursting through the door
arms laden. Imagine all this,
then imagine silence
like a prayer.

by Julianne Seeman

VIEW, TEARDOWN
San Diego, California

The chipped glass juicer, the Benny Goodman
78s, the armchair with its gouts of stuffing—
I step away from what remains inside
the house, take to the deck.
Tijuana anchors the horizon, Shelter Island's

docks hold yachts like bullets in a clip.
From the neighboring King palm tree,
birdsong rises above the roar
of Navy jets.
Oh mockingbird,

my mother's words come back, teaching
me your name in childhood: *That's a mocker.*
Blind in her last year, she heard you sing
incessantly from the same palm,
remarked, *It's a new bird, a mystery.*

The screen door slaps out front, car idles
in the red zone, my suitcase holding one thing
I did not consign to the shippers:
a four-leaf clover that fell out
of a book by a poet

named Teasdale.
My wife runs to tell me I'm late.
Mimus Polyglottoes, I finally remove
myself, so your song may bless
the swing of the wrecking ball.

by John Willson

Chapter 36: Revisioning

William Stafford said that critics don't "belong in the consciousness of the writer while he's writing." However, after writing a poem, Stafford revised. Revision is part of the process of writing. As May Sarton said, "...revision is not *going back* and fussing around, but going *forward* into the highly complex and satisfying process of creation."

Writing is a process of critical thinking. If we're lucky, once in a while one of the Muses comes in and we have a poem that's fully realized. She's come from somewhere, knock, knock, knocking, and we let her in. She sings her song and is gone, but the proof of the visitor shows in pen, pencil, or the typewritten words on the page.

When we write, we're obviously trying to say something–something somewhat important. Maybe *Very Important*. Yes, we may have learned the craft of writing. We've published, some of us. We have books, some of us. We have experience, all of us. But each new piece is a kind of birth. Those who have given birth to a child know what it took. And it wasn't necessarily easier with the second child. Or the third. Different, yes. Each new poem a poet writes comes in brand spanking new.

But once we have the poem on the page, we want to make it as strong as we can. I like to use the word *revisioning*—which isn't in the dictionary—but it connotes the idea not only of reconsidering or rethinking but of re-seeing, of being a visionary or seer.

Did Robert Frost get it right on the page the first time? Mary Oliver? Yeats? Yeats even compared remaking his poems to remaking himself. If you look up the original version of "The Waste Land" by T.S. Eliot, you will see that it is incredibly different than the poem we know today. Elizabeth Bishop's "One Art" went through fifteen different drafts before she arrived at her final poem. Ernest Hemingway rewrote the last page of *A Farewell to Arms* thirty-nine times. I don't know about the other pages, but thirty-nine times took a lot of paper and energy, since he obviously used a typewriter at the time, pounding away on the keys, one draft after another. He was not the only one who did several revisions—novelist Vladimir Nabokov said that his pencils outlasted their erasers.

When you are revising a poem, consider the following:

—Many strong poems include images and active verbs.

- —Many adverbs are not needed. Consider cutting them or use them sparingly. (Sparingly is an adverb.)
- —Look for clichés in your writing and cut or replace them.
- —Use adjectives that make a difference. "Pretty baby" won't cut it.
- —Stay clear of abstractions. Focus on concrete language, image, and meaning.

Some writers, such as Rita Dove and Katherine Patterson, love revision. Others don't but they do it. Most, like E. B. White, John Updike, William Stafford, May Sarton, and Jane Hirshfield, among many others, advise revision.

Stafford said in an interview in *The Paris Review* with William Young: "No matter how many times I go over it (the work) I don't ever feel that it's finished or that it has settled... I don't think that correctness or absolute rightness is in the realm of human possibility. So work is always revisable, as far as I'm concerned."

In an essay titled "The Problems and Delights of Revision," Sarton writes "...revision, far from being an extraneous, prim manipulation from outside, becomes a triumphant means toward growth and understanding." She also advised that writers should "Keep to the concrete. Abstract words do not make the reader experience anything specific enough..."

E. B. White extensively revised his essay on the first moon landing, which was published in *The New Yorker*. In three of the drafts, he begins with "Planning a trip to the moon differs in no essential respect from planning a trip to the beach." The drafts run 300 and more words. By the final, a 209-word paragraph, he ditches the beginning line and writes, "The moon, as it turns out, is a great place for men."

In the first draft White uses sentences of approximately the same length, mostly between 14 and 28 words. Each draft adds more varied sentence lengths. He uses words such *as dill pickles, desperately, pondered, telescoped flagpole, moon, emotion, pioneers,* and *lovers* in the first draft. In the next draft, he keeps the "pickles and desperately" but changes "pondered" to "planned" and "telescoped flagpole" to "jointed flagpole." He also kept "moon" and "lovers" in but took "pioneers" out. New words include *pride, nationalism, tides, pity, handkerchief, no borders.*

The final published version has no dill pickles. Flag has no adjective associated with it. In fact, the moon is not a good place for flags, he decides. Each draft is more specific, more didactic with more active verbs. He uses a simile in the published paragraph. His argument remains the same: "What a pity" we didn't honor this amazing achievement as more of a universal achievement, he concludes, but the final becomes less of a criticism, more of a lament.

The first draft concludes with the idea that it should have been a "white banner" we planted rather than a US flag. The published piece ends with "white handkerchief...symbol of the common cold," something that "unites us all."

Sometimes we don't know where we're going until we've headed out, landed, returned to the starting point, and headed out again–the very way we learned to walk, to talk, to find our passion and voice.

When we work on our poems, we can "revision" them in several different ways. These next exercises will require a draft of a poem already written, and will hopefully help you find some new ways to re-vision it.

(The exercises below focus on revising a previously written poem. You can use the same poem for each exercise in order to see several "revisioning" possibilities or you can use a different poem for each exercise.)

Exercise 1: Revisioning Questions To Ask Yourself

Print out a draft of a poem that you have written that you are not satisfied with. Read through your poem (writing your answers directly on the poem) as you ask these questions:

> What are you saying? Is it what you thought you said?
> What did you want to say?
> Are there images?
> Is your topic of interest to readers?
> Are there places you become bored with in your poem?
> Do certain areas feels sloppy and not well crafted?
> Where can you tighten the poem by taking out extraneous words?
> Where can you expand the poem?
> Are you using dull vocabulary and failing to surprise your reader?

Is the form working for your topic—couplets or longer stanzas?
Are you finding any spelling or grammatical errors?

Write all of your notes on the poem as you reflect on the questions above. Make edits to words, lines, punctuation, stanza format, and line breaks. Once you have completed your revision on paper, retype your poem as a new document. As you type, give yourself permission to continue to revise.

Exercise 2: Cut It Out

Print out one of your poems that you'd like to revise, and with scissors, cut out each individual line. Mix up the lines and lay them out in front of you in a new order. Begin to play with the order to see if you can create a stronger or more surprising version of your original draft. You can also do this same exercise by cutting out full stanzas of the poem and rearranging them.

Exercise 3: Tackling Problem Words

Print out a draft of your poem and circle or highlight any words you feel could be stronger or more intriguing. Look up these words in a dictionary even though you already know the meaning. Read the full definition—does it inspire you to add more to your poem based on the definition or do you realize you could choose a better word? You can also use a Thesaurus to find synonyms for your "problem" words. Once you have revised your poem, retype it in a document using your new words. If you are inspired to make more changes as you type, don't hold back.

Exercise 4: Rely On Memory

Print out a draft of a poem and read it aloud three times. Now, immediately type your poem into a word document relying on your memory as much as you can. If you can't remember a line, make up a new one. Don't worry about this new version of the poem being an exact replica of the original. When you are finished, compare your new poem to your original draft and consider which new lines might be stronger. Incorporate the best parts of your new poem into your original draft.

Exercise 5: Cross It Out

Print out a poem you would like to revise and cross out every fifth or tenth word or cross out every other line of the poem. As you reread your poem without those words/lines, how has the meaning changed? Is the poem more interesting? Revise your poem using this method or create your own scheme for eliminating words or lines. Perhaps you can cross out every seventh word or every fourth line. You may also want to focus on crossing out certain parts of speech, like third adjective, article, verb, etc.

Poems To Inspire Your Work:

Here are two examples of my first drafts and final drafts for poems. "Snowmelt" was published in *Prairie Schooner* and "Homecoming" appeared in *Poet Lore*.

First Draft:

WOULD-BE BRIDE

Decades later, when village men carried the soon-
to-be bridegroom
back during a dry season
from his hike in the mountains, she bent
      over the body,
      he still young
      and whole,
her hands calloused, back humped
from hoeing the fields and denting
one side of the mattress
where she'd curled, shriveled
with her seeds.
      When he lay
      under her fingers, his cheeks
      smooth, his fingers long and straight
her anger bloomed: how she would
      have to give him back
      to his first love.

Final Draft:

SNOWMELT

Decades later, when the village men carried
the bridegroom back from the hike
he took the day before his wedding,

    she bent over the body,
    touched his forehead, cheeks,
    his fingers long, cold - perfect still.

Something inside her stirred,
he still young and whole,
lips full.

    He lay under her arthritic hands,
    skin spotted with sun, back humped
        from hoeing the fields, her bones denting

one side of the mattress
where she'd curled around her seeds.

    And her anger bloomed.

She would have to give him back
    to his first love.

☙

First Draft:

BORGES' DREAM

The hour went sun-drunk.
Blindness spread

roots like a banyan.
He stroked

the page, the poems
out of ancient soil

"that Ithaca/of green
eternity." Words leaked

out of his fingers,
dripped fig-red. He rode

a large orange-spotted tiger
across his mind,

over a field he couldn't see,
and found shoots

on the weeping fig
he'd thought was dead.

Final Draft:

HOMECOMING

Borges ran his mind over
Everything he couldn't see, put philosophy,
Fiction and theology in the same bed

Where they bumped into each other,
Pulled the covers, argued over who should
Wash the sheets. When he went blind, letters

Walked with their hands out of his fingers, letters
Dripping fig-red on the page. He stroked the fig's bark,
Found shoots on what he thought was dead.

He stroked the page and the hour went sun-drunk.
Like a banyan tree, blindness had spread its aerial roots,
So he dictated out of ancient soil filled

With "that Ithaca/of green eternity,
Not of marvels," soil bearing a cart load of figs,
Banyans and breadfruit for the bats and birds, food

For the dream tigers riding the maze, mortals
Astride tigers talking to the Buddha,
To the un-nettable clouds

And Ulysses, who wept for his "Ithaca,
Green and humble." Borges rode a large tiger,
Orange-spotted, through the world where he lived.

Chapter 37: Concluding Thoughts—Why Poetry?

Now that you have worked through this book, take a moment to reflect on what creative writing and poetry mean in your life. Are they hobbies? Are they essential? Would your life be less without them?

Here are some thoughts on the writing process by several noted writers and poets:

Grace Paley in an interview with Jonathan Dee, Barbara Jones, and Larissa MacFarquhar in *The Paris Review* in 1992 closed the interview with the following: "The best training is to read and write, no matter what. Don't live with a lover or roommate who doesn't respect your work. Don't lie, buy time, borrow to buy time. Write what will stop your breath if you don't write."

In her book *Living Color/Painting, Writing, and the Bones of Seeing*, **Natalie Goldberg** writes in her introduction: "First, you need to understand that writing and drawing are natural human endeavors. Trees, apples, sauerkraut jars, cars, tables, lions, dolphins–none of these can write or draw. Only human beings do." In her book titled *The True Secret of Writing*, Goldberg advises, "Buy a fast pen and cheap notebook...The pen should be fast enough to keep up with your mind..."

In "A Way of Writing," **William Stafford** said that a writer "is not so much someone who has something to say as he is someone who has found a process that will bring about new things...." He concludes with what he says is a "final, dual reflection: 1. Writers may not be special...." and "2. But writing itself is one of the great, free human activities. There is scope for individuality, and elation, and discovery, in writing. For the person who follows with trust and forgiveness...the world remains always ready and deep, an inexhaustible environment, with the combined vividness of an actuality and flexibility of a dream."

Dean Young in *The Art of Recklessness: Poetry as Assertive Force and Contradiction*, wrote: "Poetry is not efficient. If you want to learn how to cook a lobster, it's probably best not to look to poetry. But if you want to see the word lobster in all its reactant oddity, its pied beauty, as if for the first time, go to poetry. And if you want to know what it's like to be that lobster in the pot, that's in poetry too."

E. B. White in his interview with George Plimpton and Frank H. Crowther for *The Paris Review* in 1969 said, "...a writer has the duty to be good, not lousy; true, not false; lively, not dull; accurate, not full of error. He should tend to lift people up, not lower them down. Writers do not merely reflect and interpret life, they inform and shape life."

I tell my students that the wonderful thing about being a writer is that nothing is lost. Anything and everything is fodder for our writing. And so it is. So it is that language dies. Memories go. But words in the books I read and my pen's scratchings on the page when I was young gave me an outlet, gave me hope. Poetry is like the stars I saw years ago in Delphi, star after star falling into the chasm by the taverna.

Concluding Exercise: Thank You

Write a letter poem to someone who has been your teacher or mentor, living or dead. Say thank you through details, dialogue, and how you, as the poet/writer, appreciate and make use of the gifts this person bestowed upon you. Be specific about *how* he/she/they taught you to write and *what* he/she/they taught you. For instance, maybe a high school teacher taught you to write by dramatically reading poetry aloud in class (the *how*) and after a year in his/her/their class, you could compose poems that captured your love of nature because you learned how to use language—"the lilies swell in the wind, swing toward the sunshadow on the cedar"—and your first poem was published before you were twenty-one (the *what*). Give your reader a picture of why this person stands out to you as a formative influence in your writing life.

The following poem is in honor of Lonny Kaneko, my first poetry teacher who came into my life when I was in my 30s. He and Carl Sandburg are why I came to call myself "poet."

DEAR LONNY KANEKO (1939-2017)

Born two years before me, you'd been loaded
in a box car, shipped with other Kanekos,
Mitsuis and Naganawas into a place eaten
by the sun, to where the sheep had left
and people, your people, were planted in the wind
and barbed corral. Your father had stood
between dignity and dust. After the war,
your mother prowled the gray foundation

of a vanished house, ribs of a barn, barren soil.
Raised on fearing evil in Ohio's rusting valley,
I heard the Great Divide calling. We both
ended up between the Cascades
and Olympics in Seattle where I found you –
after a dusty road out of Minidoka, a name
meaning water where there was no water –
where I began to trust
that I, too, would see
in the dark waiting for morning light
that each word is god.

Poems To Inspire Your Work:

LANGUAGES

There are no handles upon a language
Whereby men take hold of it
And mark it with signs for its remembrance.
It is a river, this language,
Once in a thousand years
Breaking a new course
Changing its way to the ocean.
It is mountain effluvia
Moving to valleys
And from nation to nation
Crossing borders and mixing.
Languages die like rivers.
Words wrapped round your tongue today
And broken to shape of thought
Between your teeth and lips speaking
Now and today
Shall be faded hieroglyphics
Ten thousand years from now.
Sing—and singing—remember
Your song dies and changes
And is not here to-morrow
Any more than the wind
Blowing ten thousand years ago.

by Carl Sandburg

PERFECT READER

After a dreamy recital, she stands
at the podium, disposed to take
a few questions.
Someone asks: Who is your ideal reader?
Modestly, she replies, One who reads
a poem more than once.
There and then, I vow to be her reader.
I will recite the poem until its words enter me
like a lover who waits for the silky readiness
of the beloved's lust.
I will read aloud and in silence, I will memorize
line by line. I will read ardently and get lost
time and again. I will backstroke languidly
to the beginning a million times
to locate, not her meaning, nor mine,
but ours.
Or if there is no meaning, I will
contemplate the depths of emptiness.
I will not be deterred by difficult diction
or syntax. I will chew the poem
down to its scaffolding and ink it
with red stars to navigate each of its turns.
I will not sleep or eat
during the countless hours
of our tête-á-tête.

by Risa Denenberg

SOME REASONS WHY I BECAME A POET

Because I wanted to undo each stitch
in time, unravel the nine seams
that inhibit remembering; because I wanted
to roll a stone with such tenderness
that moss would grow & hold light
on all sides at once; because I wanted to teach
every old dog I saw a new set of tricks;
because I wanted to lead a blind horse
to water & make her believe her thirst
mattered; because I wanted to count
the chickens of grief & gain before they hatched;
because I never wanted to let sleeping cats lie
in wait beneath the birdbath; because
I wanted to close the barn door after the last
horse went grazing & know that something
important was left stalled inside; because
I wanted to welcome all Greeks & the desperate
bearing of their gifts; & because I couldn't stop
keeping my poor mouth open in a sort
of continual awe, trusting that flies, like
words, would come & go in their own good time.

by Samuel Green

CONTRIBUTOR BIOS / POEM PERMISSIONS

Hiwot Adilow is an Ethiopian-American poet from Philadelphia. "Guddu's Girl" previously published in *In the House of My Father* (Two Sylvias Press).

Kelli Russell Agodon's most recent book is *Hourglass Museum* (White Pine Press). "Funeral Perfume" was previously published in *Red Mountain Review*.

Former Washington State poet laureate **Elizabeth Austen** is at work on her next collection, *States of Emergency*. "How To Vote Like a Girl" originally published as "How to Write Like a Girl" at the *Rise Up Review*. "This Morning" originally published in *Pontoon 7*. "In Praise of Orality" originally published in the Jack Straw Writers anthology, 2003.

Deborah Bacharach is the author of *After I Stop Lying* (Cherry Grove Publications). "As We Float Towards the Pacific, the Clouds Appear Heartshaped" used with permission from the author.

Jamaica Baldwin is a published poet and scholar living in Lincoln, NE where she is pursuing a PhD in Creative Writing. You can visit her at: www.jamaicabaldwin.wordpress.com. "re-Branding" first published as a broadside by Chatwin Books in Seattle. "What I Know" and "A Brief and Sordid History of the Speculum" were used with permission from the author.

Janée J. Baugher is the author of the ekphrastic poetry collections, *The Body's Physics* (Tebot Bach, 2013) and *Coördinates of Yes* (Ahadada Books, 2010) and the textbook, *Ekphrastic Writing: A Guide to Visual-Art-Influenced Poetry, Fiction, and Nonfiction* (McFarland, 2020). "L'Escargot" previously published in *Coördinates of Yes* (Ahadada Books).

Michele Bombardier is the author of *What We Do* (2018), a Hedgebrook fellow, and the founder of Fishplate Poetry, which offers workshops and retreats. "Aphasia Testing" first published in *Bellevue Literary Review* as well as her full-length collection, *What We Do* (Kelsay Books). "On The Ten Year Anniversary Of A Friend's Death" used with permission from the author.

Elizabeth Bradfield is the author of four books, most recently *Toward Antarctica*. Founder and editor-in-chief of Broadsided Press, she lives on Cape Cod, works as a naturalist on ships and shores around the globe, and is Associate Professor of creative writing at Brandeis University. "Regarding the Absent Heat of Your Skin on Letters I Receive While at Sea" previously published in *Alaska Quarterly Review*. "Capillary Action" previously published in *Rethinking History*.

Traci Brimhall is the author of four books of poetry, most recently of *Come the Slumberless to the Land of Nod* (Copper Canyon Press). "Love Poem Without a Drop of Hyperbole" was previously published in *The New Yorker*.

Poet and photographer, **Ronda Piszk Broatch** is the author of *Lake of Fallen Constellations*, (MoonPath Press), and a lover of writing surrealist poems with wine and chocolate. "There Are So Many Things" previously published in *Bracken Magazine* and "A Stone in the Road" previously published in *Dogwood*.

Catalina Marie Cantú, a Jack Straw Fellow with poetry published in *La Bloga*, *Poetry on Buses*, and *Raven Chronicles* is current President/co-founder of La Sala, a Latinx artist collective. "Reflections on Home/ Reflexiones en Casa" previously published on *Poetry on the Buses*. "Buelita" previously published in *Raven Chronicles*,

Pamela Hobart Carter has two degrees in geology and loves how close she lives to active volcanoes. "Her Father Was a Pair of Binoculars in This Metaphor" previously published in *Tilde, a literary journal*.

Cheryl Clayton is an aspiring poet living on a ranch in west Texas. "Eleven" was used with permission from the author.

Kelly Cressio-Moeller is a poet and editor living in San Jose, CA; visit her website at www.kellycressiomoeller.com to read more. "Viva La Vida" previously published *Hermeneutic Chaos Literary Journal*.

John Davis, the author of *Gigs* and a chapbook, *The Reservist*, lives on an island in Puget Sound and has published over 400 poems. "Judge a Book By Its Cover" and "Dance of the Presidential Debate" used with the permission from the author.

Lauren Davis is the author of *Each Wild Thing's Consent* (Poetry Wolf Press). "Every Sunday at the Grocery Store" previously published in *Tar River Poetry*.

Risa Denenberg is a writer, editor, reviewer, and publisher of poetry. "Perfect Reader" previously published in *Whirlwind @ Lesbos* (Headmistress Press).

"There Came a Wind Like a Bugle" by **Emily Dickinson** is in the public domain.

Suzanne Edison writes most often about the intersections of illness, medicine, science, healing and art. She teaches at Hugo House and lives in Seattle. "The Magician" previously published in *What Cannot Be Swallowed*.

"Solution" by **Ralph Waldo Emerson** is in the public domain.

Jeannine Hall Gailey served as the second Poet Laureate of Redmond, WA and is the author of five books of poetry and the nonfiction book *PR for Poets*. "Horoscope" previously published in *Rattle*. "Green Willow Wife" previously published in *She Returns From the Floating World* (Two Sylvias Press).

Lea Galanter is a Seattle-area editor and writer. "Degrees of White in Washington" used with permission from the author.

Carmen Gillespie is an English professor, director of the Griot Institute and the author of a chapbook, three poetry collections, *Jonestown: A Vexation*, *The Blue Black Wet of Wood*, and *The Ghosts of Monticello: A Recitatif*, and three literary critical books, *A Critical Companion to Toni Morrison*, *A Critical Companion to Alice Walker*, and *Toni Morrison: Forty Years in the Clearing*. "The earth is loud" previously published in *The Blue Black of Wood* (Two Sylvias Press).

Jennifer Givhan is a Mexican-American poet who has earned NEA and PEN/Rosenthal Emerging Voices fellowships and published four full-length collections of poetry, most recently *Rosa's Einstein* (University of Arizona Press). "At the Altar of Staying" previously published in *Girl With Death Mask* (Blue Lights Books / Indiana University Press).

Samuel Green's most recent collection of poems is *All That Might Be Done* (Carnegie-Mellon University Press, 2014). "Old Man Folding a Kerchief in the Supermarket" and "Some Reasons Why I Became a Poet" are reprinted with permission from *The Grace of Necessity*, (Carnegie Mellon University Press, 2008) Copyright © 2008 by Samuel Green.

Netter Hansen lives in Seattle where she writes fiction, non-fiction, and poetry. "The White Rope" previously published in *Signs of Life*.

Sharon Hashimoto, who also writes fiction, will have her book of poems, *The Crane Wife*, re-published by Red Hen Press. "In Hawaii, We Do This," previously published in *PONTOON*. "A Walk Along the Snohomish" previously published in *The Written Arts* and *The Crane Wife* (Story Line Press). "At the Foulweather Bluff Preserve" used with permission from the author.

Holly J. Hughes is the author of two collections of poetry, most recently *Passings*, which received an American Book Award in 2017, the co-author of *The Pen & The Bell: Mindful Writing in a Busy World* and the editor of *Beyond Forgetting: Poetry & Prose about Alzheimer's Disease*. You can visit her at: www.hollyjhughes.com "Cape Disappointment" previously published in Windfall.

Tom C. Hunley is a professor in the MFA/BA Creative Writing programs at Western Kentucky University, a father of four, and author, most recently, of *What Feels Like Love: New And Selected Poems* (C&R Press). "Musives and a Silent Crump" previously published in *TriQuarterly* and *Jump Start* (Steel Toe Press).

Jennifer Jean is the author of *The Fool* (Big Table), the recipient of a 2018 Disquiet Fellowship to Portugal and a 2017 Her Story Is residency in Dubai, and she teaches Free2Write Poetry Workshops to sex-trafficking survivors. "Malibu Beach" previously published in *The Common*.

Lois P. Jones is the author of *Night Ladder* (Glass Lyre Press), Poetry Editor of the Pushcart Prize winning *Kyoto Journal*, host of Southern California's Poets Café on KPFK, winner of the Bristol Poetry Prize among others and has published in numerous journals and anthologies with work forthcoming in *New Voices: Contemporary Writers Confronting the Holocaust* (Vallentine Mitchell of London). "Four Nights in the Misty Fjords" previous published in *Altadena Poetry Review* and *Night Ladder* (Glass Lyre Press).

Susan Jostrom is a freelance writer and editor, living in Seattle, who also blogs at www.mjostrom.wordpress.com. "Remnants" used with permission from the author.

Lonny Kaneko received local and national awards, including a fellowship from the National Endowment for the Arts, for his poetry, fiction, and plays. His last book of poems *Coming Home From Camp and Other Poems* was published by Endicott and Hugh Books in 2015. "Agoraphobia: After Camp," "Sadness Is Not a River," and "Is Love a Moment Lost in Vertigo" previously published in *Coming Home from Camp and Other Poems* (Endicott and Hugh Books).

Tina Kelley's fourth book of poetry, *Rise Wildly*, is forthcoming from CavanKerry Press. "Dispatch From The Office Of The Creator Of Words" previously published in *The Journal of New Jersey Poets* and *Ardor* (winner of Jacar Press Chapbook Award).

Lynn Knight has published short stories and is currently working on a novel. "Stone" used with permission from the author.

Jenifer Browne Lawrence writes at the foot of the Olympic Mountains in Washington, and is the author of *Grayling* (Perugia Press) and *One Hundred Steps from Shore* (Blue Begonia Press). "Candling" previously published in *North American Review* (2014) and in *Grayling* (Perugia Press, 2015).

Gary Copeland Lilley is a North Carolina poet who now lives, writes, and plays music in the Pacific Northwest peninsula. "Driving At Night Towards The Hood Canal," "Standing on the Corner When Being Cool Went Blind" previously published in *The Bushman's Medicine Show* (Lost Horse Press).

Karen Lorene, writer, jewelry art authority, Antiques Roadshow appraiser is now working on her sixth book: *Retail/Detail*. "Light Gone" used with permission of the poet.

Claudia Castro Luna lives in English and Spanish, writes poems and creative non-fiction, serves as Washington State Poet Laureate and whenever possible rides a strawberry red bicycle. "María Saturnina Sultry Yearning" previously published in *Killing Marias* (Two Sylvias Press).

Jennifer Martelli is the author of *My Tarantella* from Bordighera Press and co-poetry editor for *The Mom Egg Review*. "Low-/Tide Heart of Mine" previously published in *r.kv.ry Quarterly Literary Journal*.

Robert McNamara has published three books of poetry, most recently *Incomplete Strangers* (Lost Horse Press). "Not the Stars" previously published in *The Sow's Ear Poetry Review*. "Emptying the Closet" and "Greengrocer" appeared in *Incomplete Strangers* (Lost Horse Press). "From a Window" used with permission from the author.

Author of four poetry collections, **Natasha Kochicheril Moni** is a licensed naturopathic doctor in WA State and a medical writer. "We Speak of Water" previously published in *Toasted Cheese Literary Journal* and *The Cardiologist's Daughter* (Two Sylvias Press).

Arlene Naganawa's work has appeared in *Crab Creek Review, Barnstorm, All the Sins, Pontoon, Calyx* and other publications. "The Pointed Trees" appears in the chapbook, *The Ark and the Bear* (Floating Bridge Press). "A Thing I Knew" appears in the chapbook, *The Scarecrow Bride* (Red Bird Chapbooks, 2015).

Aimee Nezhukumatathil is the author of four books of poetry, a forthcoming book of nature essays, and is professor of English in The University of Mississippi's MFA program. "The Secret of Soil" previously published in *Fire On Her Tongue: An Anthology of Contemporary Women's Poetry* (Two Sylvias Press).

January Gill O'Neil is the author of *Rewilding* (2018), *Misery Islands* (2014), and *Underlife* (2009), published by CavanKerry Press. "Body Politic" previously published in *Fire On Her Tongue: An Anthology of Contemporary Women's Poetry* (Two Sylvias Press).

Bev Osband lives in Seattle, WA, where she writes, teaches, paints watercolors, gardens, walks, knits & bakes. "When I consider everything that grows" used with permission from the author.

Mary Peelen is the author of *Quantum Heresies*, winner of the Kithara Book Prize (Glass Lyre Press). "Supernova" previously published in *Radar Poetry*.

Alison Pelegrin is the author of four poetry collections and two sons, and serves as caretaker for a trio of rescued animals in her home in south Louisiana. "Poem Folded into a Boat and Offered to the Bogue Falaya" previously published in *Waterlines* (LSU Press).

"Acrostic" by **Edgar Allan Poe** is in the public domain.

"Muse" by **Alexander Sergeyevich Pushkin** is in the public domain.

Robin Reagler writes poems from Houston, Texas, where she is the Executive Director of Writers in the Schools (WITS). "We Holy Thieves" previously published in *Teeth & Teeth* (Headmistress Press).

Seattle poet **Susan Rich** is the author of four poetry collections including *Cloud Pharmacy* and *The Alchemist's Kitchen* (White Pine Press); her awards include an Artists Trust Fellowship, Fulbright Fellowship to South Africa, and PEN USA Award. "Different Places to Pray" previously published in *The Alchemist's Kitchen* (White Pine Press). "Invitation to Mr. W" previously published in *Cures Include Travel* (White Pine Press). "Pomegranate, Radio On" previously published in *Helen: A Literary Magazine*.

Katrina Roberts draws, writes, teaches & makes whisky in Walla Walla, Washington, where she's published four books of poems & edited the anthology *Because You Asked: A Book of Answers on the Art & Craft of the Writing Life*; visit her website at www.katrinaroberts.net. "Pursuits" previously published in *Friendly Fire* (Lost Horse Press).

"Languages" by **Carl Sandburg** is in the public domain.

Heidi Seaborn is the author of *Give a Girl Chaos {see what she can do}* from C&R Press/Mastodon Books, 2019 and Editorial Director of *The Adroit Journal*. "How to Hold a Heart" previously published in *Literary and Arts Review*.

Julianne Seeman taught creative writing at Bellevue College. Her first book *Enough Light to See* won the Anhinga award and was published by U of Florida State Press. "Union Station" and "At the Sheldon Jackson Museum" used with permission from the author.

Peggy Shumaker's newest book is *Cairn, New and Selected* (Red Hen Press). "The Apple" previously published in *The Agni Review* and in *Cairn, New and Selected*

Martha Silano is the author of *Gravity Assist* (Saturnalia Books), as well as four previous poetry collections. "Shoes Like Snow" and "In The Self-Help Aisle" previously published in *What The Truth Tastes Like* (Two Sylvias Press).

Michael Spence, who drove buses in the Seattle area for thirty years, won The New Criterion Poetry Prize for his fifth book, *Umbilical*. "Umbilical" was first published in *The New Criterion*; "Broken Sonnet: Divorce" first appeared in *The Yale Review*. Both are included in his book, *Umbilical* (St. Augustine's Press, 2016).

Ann Spiers is Vashon Island's inaugural Poet Laureate and steward of its Poetry Post. You can visit her at: www.annspiers.com "American Lake" previously published in *Crab Creek Review*. "Girl" used with permission from the author.

Lisa Gluskin Stonestreet is the author of *The Greenhouse* and *Tulips, Water, Ash*. "Super Baby Jumbo Prawn" appeared in *Tulips, Water, Ash* (Northeastern University Press).

Melissa Studdard is the author of the poetry collection *I Ate the Cosmos for Breakfast* and the young adult novel *Six Weeks to Yehidah*. "I Fell In Love With a Double-Yolk Egg" previously published in *Life and Legends* and appears in *I Ate the Cosmos For Breakfast* (Saint Julian Press).

Mary Ellen Talley's poems have recently been published in *Raven Chronicles, Banshee, Flatbush Review* and *Ekphrastic Review* as well as in anthologies, *All We Can Hold* and *Ice Cream Poems*. "Pleappy" used with permission from the author.

Alexandra Teague is the author of three books of poetry—*Or What We'll Call Desire, The Wise and Foolish Builders,* and *Mortal Geography*—as well as co-editor of *Bullets into Bells: Poets & Citizens Respond to Gun Violence*. "Coyotes" previously featured on Broadsides on the Bus.

Kathryn Thurber-Smith is a social worker at Seattle Children's Hospital whose poetry has been featured in *Suisun Valley Review* and *The Grinnell Review*. "Instead of death I choose" used with permission from the author.

Lena Khalaf Tuffaha is the author of *Water & Salt*, winner of the 2018 Washington State Book Award, *Arab in Newsland*, winner of the 2016 Two Sylvia's Chapbook Prize and *Letters from the Interior*, forthcoming from Diode Press. "May Flowers" previously published in *Arab in Newsland* (Two Sylvias Press).

Cindy Veach is the author of *Gloved Against Blood* (CavanKerry Press) and the co-poetry editor of *The Mom Egg Review*. "Rose of Jericho" was originally published in Poem-a-Day by the Academy of American Poets.

John Willson, whose full-length collection, *Call This Room a Station*, was published by MoonPath Press, lives on Bainbridge Island, WA, where he has been designated an Island Treasure for outstanding contributions to arts in the community. "Love Notes" previously published in *The Sow's Ear Poetry Review*. "View, Teardown" and "Huaqueros" previously published in *The Coachella Review*.

Sandra Yannone's debut collection of poetry, *Boats for Women*, arrived in 2019 from Salmon Poetry (Ireland); for more information about her and her poetry, visit her website at: www.sandrayannone.com. "Voice Over" used with permission from the author.

190

A writer and award-winning photographer, Susan Landgraf has published more than 400 poems, essays, and articles in numerous journals and magazines. Most recently her poems have appeared, or are forthcoming, in *Prairie Schooner, Poet Lore, Nimrod, Calyx, The Bellingham Review, Literary Mama, Kestrel, Margie*, and *The Sow's Ear*.

Her full-length poetry collection *What We Bury Changes the Ground* was published by Tebot Bach in 2017. *Other Voices*, a chapbook, was published by Finishing Line Press; and a textbook, *Student Reflection Journal for Student Success*, was published by Prentice Hall.

Landgraf has given more than 150 writing workshops, and her honors include two Pushcart Prize nominations; Pablo Neruda, Society of Humanistic Anthropology, and Academy of American Poets awards; a Jack Straw Productions grant; Centrum, Hedgebrook, Ragdale, Soapstone, Whiteley, Willard R. Espy, and Willapa Bay Writers in Residence residencies; and a Theodore Morrison scholarship at Bread Loaf.

Landgraf worked as a reporter and photographer for seven years. After earning her Bachelor's and MFA degrees at the University of Washington, she taught writing, journalism, media, literature, Diversity and Globalism, and college studies for 27 years at Highline College. Through an exchange program between Highline and Shanghai Jiao Tong University, she taught at SJTU in 2002, 2008, 2010 and 2012.

Retired from full-time teaching, she serves now on the Highline Foundation Board and spends time with her family and friends; she logs in some 40-60 hours a week writing, leading workshops, and being part of several writing groups.

Publications by Two Sylvias Press:

The Daily Poet: Day-By-Day Prompts For Your Writing Practice
by Kelli Russell Agodon and Martha Silano (Print and eBook)

The Daily Poet Companion Journal (Print)

Fire On Her Tongue: An Anthology of Contemporary Women's Poetry
edited by Kelli Russell Agodon and Annette Spaulding-Convy (Print and eBook)

The Poet Tarot and Guidebook: A Deck Of Creative Exploration (Print)

The Inspired Poet: Writing Exercises To Spark New Work
by Susan Landgraf (Print and eBook)

Where The Horse Takes Wing: The Uncollected Poems of Madeline DeFrees
edited by Anne McDuffie (Print and eBook)

In The House Of My Father
Winner of the 2017 Two Sylvias Press Chapbook Prize
by Hiwot Adilow (Print and eBook)

Box, Winner of the 2017 Two Sylvias Press Poetry Prize
by Sue D. Burton (Print and eBook)

Tsigan: The Gypsy Poem (New Edition)
by Cecilia Woloch (Print and eBook)

PR For Poets
by Jeannine Hall Gailey (Print and eBook)

Appalachians Run Amok, Winner of the 2016 Two Sylvias Press Wilder Prize
by Adrian Blevins (Print and eBook)

Pass It On!
by Gloria J. McEwen Burgess (Print)

Killing Marias
by Claudia Castro Luna (Print and eBook)

The Ego and the Empiricist, Finalist 2016 Two Sylvias Press Chapbook Prize
by Derek Mong (Print and eBook)

The Authenticity Experiment
by Kate Carroll de Gutes (Print and eBook)

Mytheria, Finalist 2015 Two Sylvias Press Wilder Prize
by Molly Tenenbaum (Print and eBook)

Arab in Newsland , Winner of the 2016 Two Sylvias Press Chapbook Prize
by Lena Khalaf Tuffaha (Print and eBook)

The Blue Black Wet of Wood, Winner of the 2015 Two Sylvias Press Wilder Prize
by Carmen R. Gillespie (Print and eBook)

Fire Girl: Essays on India, America, and the In-Between
by Sayantani Dasgupta (Print and eBook)

Blood Song
by Michael Schmeltzer (Print and eBook)

Naming The No-Name Woman, Winner of the 2015 Two Sylvias Press Chapbook Prize
by Jasmine An (Print and eBook)

Community Chest
by Natalie Serber (Print)

Phantom Son: A Mother's Story of Surrender
by Sharon Estill Taylor (Print and eBook)

What The Truth Tastes Like
by Martha Silano (Print and eBook)

landscape/heartbreak
by Michelle Peñaloza (Print and eBook)

Earth, Winner of the 2014 Two Sylvias Press Chapbook Prize
by Cecilia Woloch (Print and eBook)

The Cardiologist's Daughter
by Natasha Kochicheril Moni (Print and eBook)

She Returns to the Floating World
by Jeannine Hall Gailey (Print and eBook)

Hourglass Museum
by Kelli Russell Agodon (eBook)

Cloud Pharmacy
by Susan Rich (eBook)

Dear Alzheimer's: A Caregiver's Diary & Poems
by Esther Altshul Helfgott (eBook)

Listening to Mozart: Poems of Alzheimer's
by Esther Altshul Helfgott (eBook)

Crab Creek Review 30th Anniversary Issue featuring Northwest Poets
edited by Kelli Russell Agodon and Annette Spaulding-Convy (eBook)

Please visit Two Sylvias Press (www.twosylviaspress.com) for information on purchasing our print books, eBooks, writing tools, and for submission guidelines for our annual book prizes.

www.ingramcontent.com/pod-product-compliance
Lightning Source LLC
Chambersburg PA
CBHW030111100526
44591CB00009B/364